Nathaniel Hawthorne's
THE SCARLET LETTER

Charles Leavitt

Associate Professor of English
Montclair State College

1997 Barnes & Noble Books

MACMILLAN is a registered trademark of Macmillan, Inc.
Monarch and colophons are trademarks of Simon & Schuster, Inc.,
registered in the U.S. Patent and Trademark Office.

Macmillan Publishing USA
A division of Simon & Schuster, Inc.
1633 Broadway
New York, NY 10019

ISBN 0-7607-0580-1

Text design by Tony Meisel

Printed and bound in the United States of America.

99 00 01 M 9 8 7 6 5

RRDC

CONTENTS

INTRODUCTION

BRIEF ACCOUNT OF HAWTHORNE'S LIFE

Nathaniel Hawthorne was born on Independence Day, 1804, in Salem, Massachusetts, the son and grandson of sea captains. Hawthorne's ancestors had been in Salem for a good part of two hundred years. They came to the New World with Governor Winthrop in 1603. His first two famous ancestors in America were William, a stern persecutor of the Quakers, and William's son John, one of the three judges at the Salem witch trials in 1692. When Hawthorne was four years old, his father died in Dutch Guiana during a long sea voyage. The boy's poverty-stricken mother moved herself, Nathaniel, and his two sisters, Elizabeth and Maria Louisa, to the home of relatives in Salem. At the age of about nine, he suffered an injury to his foot. Because he was confined at home for several years, he had time to read many books, especially the works of Sir Walter Scott, John Bunyan, and Shakespeare. As the years passed, Nathaniel was a frequent visitor in an uncle's home at Raymond, Maine (near Lake Sebago), where he enjoyed outdoor life. Finally, his family moved to Raymond when he was about fourteen years old.

After preparing for college with a tutor in Salem, Nathaniel entered Bowdoin College, in Brunswick, Maine, from which he was graduated with the class of 1825. Returning to Salem, he spent practically all of his time perfecting the art of writing. He finished and had published in 1828 a novel, *Fanshawe,* a poorly disguised picture of college life as he had seen it at Bowdoin. He decided that his best form of expression in literature was the tale (what we call the short story). He wrote a number of short tales during this period, many of them published in magazines or in "token" books (gift books for special occasions or holidays). The years from 1825 to 1836 have been called by some critics the "twelve solitary years," for he stayed in Salem much of the time, traveled only slightly, and had few friends.

In 1837, he published his first collection of stories, *Twice Told Tales*. Although the book received good reviews, he did not earn the money he had hoped to. At this time, he met Sophia Peabody (a sort of American Elizabeth Barrett Browning), and the couple became engaged in 1838. To earn money, Hawthorne worked as measurer in the Boston Custom House from 1839 to 1840. For six months in 1841, he lived at Brook Farm, a communal project (which he used as the basis of his long work of fiction, *The Blithedale Romance*). In 1842, he married Sophia Peabody, and the two settled in the "Old Manse" in Concord. The second volume of *Twice-Told Tales* was published during this year and received a very complimentary review by Edgar Allan Poe. For three and a half years, Hawthorne and his wife lived extremely happily in Concord, where on very little money they read, wrote, talked, and in general enjoyed life. They liked the company of their Concord neighbors, especially Ralph Waldo Emerson and Henry David Thoreau. In 1846, three important things happened in Hawthorne's life: his son Julian was born; he published a collection of tales written in Concord, titled *Mosses from an Old Manse;* and he accepted a well-paying position as surveyor at the Salem Custom House. In 1849, the Whigs came into office with Zachary Taylor's election as president. A faithful Democrat, Hawthorne lost his job, according to the principles of the "spoils system" (to the political victor go the "spoils"). Hawthorne gloomily settled down to finish writing *The Scarlet Letter,* a novel he had casually begun back in 1847. *The Scarlet Letter* was published in 1850, and is still considered one of the greatest American novels. In the same year, he moved to Lenox, Massachusetts, where he settled down with his family in a "little red house." There he wrote *The House of the Seven Gables,* a study in hereditary consequences of evil, set in Salem. This appeared in 1851. While in Lenox, he was friendly with Herman Melville, who dedicated *Moby-Dick* (1851) to Hawthorne. Later in that year, Hawthorne and his family (now complete with three children) journeyed to eastern Massachusetts, where they settled for a winter in West

Newton. Here he wrote the least successful of his four major long works of fiction, *The Blithedale Romance,* a study of a socialist community, based upon his stay at Brook Farm.

In 1852, he bought a home in Concord named "The Wayside," where he wrote the presidential campaign biography for his Bowdoin College friend, Franklin Pierce. The Democrats won the election, and a grateful Pierce appointed Hawthorne United States consul in Liverpool, England. From 1853 to 1857, the Hawthornes were in England. He found time to travel throughout parts of the British Isles, recording his impressions in journals, which have been published as the *English Notebooks.* From 1858 to 1859, the Hawthornes were in Italy, where he gathered much material, some of which was published later as the *Italian Notebooks,* and some of which became the background of his last complete novel, *The Marble Faun.* This last book, a long and detailed study of good and evil, and of Americans in Europe, was published in 1860. Returning to America in the same year, he settled with his family in Concord, where his health began to fail. His writing powers decreased, although he was able to incorporate some of the material of the English journals into a book of excellent essays about England, *Our Old Home.* Toward the end of his life he suffered rapid deterioration, and he died on May 19, 1864, while on a trip to the White Mountains of New Hampshire with his friend Franklin Pierce.

HAWTHORNE'S THEORY OF ROMANCE

A major reason why Hawthorne occupies an important and individual place in the literature of the entire world is his mastery of that form of fiction known as the romance. How is Hawthorne's concept of romance different from and better than that of others? Of course, he incorporates some of the usual ideas characteristic of romanticism, such as adventurous action, heroic characters (bigger than those found in ordinary life), or picturesque (unusual) settings and characters. He even includes mysterious events, as well as scenes and ideas that are generally considered remote (or distant) from everyday, common life. But he does more. In *The Scarlet Letter,* he writes on serious topics that reveal the "truth of the human heart." Then, he chooses as his settings places "a little removed from the highway of ordinary travel," where his imaginary characters may play their parts without being exposed to too "close a comparison with the actual event of real lives." (Hawthorne does not wish his characters and their actions to be confused with specific, real-life characters and actions.) His next step is to choose characters who have actually lived and mix them in with fictitious characters (people his imagination tells him might have lived). Having chosen his setting and his characters, his next step is to describe them so that they become a strange mixture of the real and the unreal. This brings us to the most outstanding characteristic of his technique, what he calls the management of his "atmospherical medium" so as "to bring out or mellow the lights and deepen and enrich the shadows of the picture." He is concerned with something that is very important in theater and art—the lights. He realizes that as light on a stage is increased or decreased, there is a change in the atmosphere of the piece. The contrast in light and shade is called *chiaroscuro.* (Consider the use of darkness in horror films. Take an ordinary room in a house with which we are very familiar. Turn the lights down low, and suddenly there appear shadows that can frighten us or maybe just excite our imaginations. Think about how the garments in a poorly lighted closet somehow look different to us from the way they do when they are viewed in the direct, full light of day.) Accordingly, Hawthorne chooses his "atmospherical medium" (whether it is sunlight, moonlight, or firelight) and allows this "medium" to bathe (or cover) ordinary objects or scenes. The result is strikingly different. Describing his deserted parlor in the Old Manse in Concord, Hawthorne declares that the light of the moon "in a familiar room" falls "white upon the carpet . . . showing all its figures so distinctively . . . so minutely visible," that the rug and everything else in the room are changed or "spiritualized by the unusual light." The room now has a "quality of strangeness and remoteness," even though it is nearly as light as it might be by daylight. At this point, Hawthorne arrives at his destination. Because of the lighting, the "familiar room has become a neutral territory, somewhere between the real world and fairy-land, where the Actual and the Imaginary may meet," with each borrowing from and adding to the other. "Ghosts might enter here" without frightening one. Then he concludes his discussion of romance with the comment that looking glasses in a room dimly lighted by moonlight or firelight remove a romanticist one step "further from the actual, and nearer to the imagination."

The Scarlet Letter is a romance. Hester's adultery, based on love and passion, may be called romantic. The main themes of hypocrisy and revenge are serious topics. The interior of the human heart is probed. Conscience and remorse are serious matters for speculation. The setting (seventeenth-century Boston and the scaffold) is quite unrelated to the experience of readers. The characters are a mixture, from the world of the living (Governor Bellingham and Reverend John Wilson) and from the author's imagination (Hester Prynne, Arthur Dimmesdale, Roger Chillingworth, and Pearl). The management of the "atmospherical medium" (chiaroscuro) is very effective. The first scaffold scene takes place in the intense daylight of noon—Hester is clearly seen by all. The second scaffold scene takes place in the dark of night—Dimmesdale holding Hester and Pearl's hands is not visible to people. The third scaffold scene occurs in the daytime—all can clearly see the minister on the scaffold, and Dimmesdale confesses in the clear light of day, hiding nothing. Notice the moral implication involved in light and darkness: the light of day reveals evil; the darkness hides wickedness and cowardice. Another aspect of chiaroscuro is the use of sunlight. Pearl is pleased that it often surrounds her in play. Hester (symbolizing departure from virtue) arrives on the scene, and the sun disappears. The glare of the meteor lights up the landscape, revealing the lovers and their child on the scaffold at night. The numerous mirrors (such as the reflecting breastplate of the suit of armor and the pools of water into which Pearl looks) add rich and varied layers of meaning to the romantic actions, characters, and scenes in *The Scarlet Letter.*

LITERARY TECHNIQUES USED IN THE SCARLET LETTER

Hawthorne employs some remarkably varied literary techniques in his writing. The following are most important.

THE GOTHIC NOVEL OF TERROR AND WONDER

Hawthorne is fascinated by the many devices of the Gothic novel, including: (1) the manuscript: a literary trick whereby the author attempts to convince the reader that the source of the story is actually being revealed by a document, such as Surveyor Pue's "small roll of dingy paper" tied together with a rag of scarlet cloth in the form of the letter *A,* described in "The Custom House"; (2) the gloomy and dismal castle, with its haunted staircase: suggestive of Hester's dark prison and Governor Bellingham's elaborately decorated mansion; (3) the crime: such as Hester's adultery, a crime punishable by death according to Puritan law; (4) religion: represented by the Puritan ministers, the Reverend Arthur Dimmesdale and the Reverend John Wilson, as well as the Apostle Eliot; (5) Italians: pictured in the Gothic novel as dark-featured individuals beyond the bounds of ordinary law and order, represented in *The Scarlet Letter* by the sailors—"rough-looking desperadoes"—with their exotic clothing and lusty manners; (6) deformity: Roger Chillingworth has one shoulder higher than the other; (7) ghosts: the "diabolical shapes" Arthur Dimmesdale sees in the looking glass during his long night watches; (8) magic: hinted at by Mistress Hibbins—who is later "executed as a witch"—when she tells of the activities of the Black Man of the forest; (9) nature: the use of "natural phenomena," like the "red letter in the sky," which Dimmesdale sees in the shape of an *A* for adultery; (10) armored knights and helmets:

the "convex mirrors" formed by both the breastplate and the headpiece of the suit of armor in Governor Bellingham's hall; also the procession of elaborately dressed soldiers marching to music during the "New England Holiday"; (11) works of art: the symbolic biblical tapestry in Dimmesdale's apartment concerning David, Bathsheba, and Nathan the Prophet; and (12) blood: the horrifying "red stigma"—the unhealed wound—on Dimmesdale's breast.

PSYCHOLOGICAL CONFLICT

Unlike many writers of fiction who picture only surface details, Hawthorne analyzes the inward tensions of his characters. Dimmesdale, the hypocrite, is filled with remorse as he keeps reviewing in his mind his guilt. His sensitive conscience forces him to keep midnight watches. Chillingworth becomes a "fiend" as he pursues his psychological revenge on Dimmesdale. Hester, outwardly subdued by the Puritans, continues to speculate on the place of women in the world.

AN ABSTRACT MORAL IDEA
SUPPORTED BY SPECIFIC DETAILS

In the forest, Dimmesdale tells Hester, in reference to Chillingworth, "That old man's revenge has been blacker than my sin." He is referring to the devilish torture the "fiend" Chillingworth has put him through, in contrast to his lesser sin of hypocrisy (not revealing that he is Pearl's father). Much of the action of the story is built around the details of Chillingworth's vengeance.

ROMANCE

Romance, chiaroscuro, and the managing of the "atmospherical medium" are discussed above.

ASSOCIATIONAL PSYCHOLOGY

Knowing that specific places are connected with certain emotions and attitudes already well established in the mind of the reader, Hawthorne refers to Boston locales (such as King's

Chapel), leading Boston magistrates (such as Governors Bellingham and Winthrop), and Puritan standards of conduct (such as deep reverence for the ministry). The reader does not need some of the historical details filled in, for he or she knows these facts through a knowledge of history.

THE INDIRECT METHOD

Often Hawthorne does not tell the reader exactly what the answer to a question is. He offers numerous solutions and then allows the reader to decide for himself or herself. Consider the "various explanations" of the "red stigma" on Dimmesdale's breast in Chapter XXIV. Three different theories suggest how the mark happened to be there, and one theory explains that it was not there at all.

SYMBOLISM

The Scarlet Letter is rich in symbolism, a concern with double meanings where a physical object suggests a moral quality or abstract idea. The title itself keynotes the book. Hester wears a scarlet letter *A* to indicate publicly that she is an adulteress, a scarlet woman. The rose at the end of Chapter I is a symbol or token that nature can be kind, even if people are unkind to man. The scaffold is a symbol of Puritan justice or enforcement of the laws. Governor Bellingham in his elaborate garments is a symbol of the leadership and might and power of the entire colony. The word "leech" is an ancient word for physician, but Hawthorne cleverly chooses it for its double meaning, for it also stands for a person who preys on another for gain—in general terms, a good description of Chillingworth and his relationship with Dimmesdale. Pearl, brilliantly dressed, is a living symbol of Hester's sin. She is also called a jewel, purchased at great price. The "red stigma" on Dimmesdale's breast symbolizes the unhappy minister's remorse and conscience. The red meteor in the sky in the form of the letter *A,* as seen by Dimmesdale, symbolizes to him the act of adultery. (The point is made that another guilty person "might have seen another symbol in it.") Dimmesdale represents all earthly goodness to his congregation. On the other hand, old Mistress Hibbins is a token of all the unknown deviltry connected with the dreaded Black Man of the forest.

SPECIALIZED TECHNIQUES BORROWED FROM SIR WALTER SCOTT

There are three devices, in particular, that Hawthorne borrows from the great English romancer: (1) The "unknown" character (often called the stranger) appears in the story and helps to complicate the plot. Later in the tale he is unveiled, but generally for a long time the mystery of his identity helps create suspense. Chillingworth, of course, is the "unknown" character in *The Scarlet Letter.* Although the reader early in the book knows who he really is (Dr. Prynne, Hester's husband), Dimmesdale does not know it. (2) The caricature of minor characters, sometimes for humorous purposes. A caricature is a description of a person in which certain features of speech, dress, or personality are exaggerated or distorted so as to produce an absurd effect. Mistress Hibbins, with her elaborate clothing and her frequent remarks about the Black Man of the forest, is a caricature. (3) The use of elaborately detailed scenes planned on a huge scale. The first scaffold scene, the "New England Holiday" festivities, and the third scaffold scene where Dimmesdale confesses are examples.

TECHNIQUES OF THE THEATER

Hawthorne adopts a theatrical point of view. Often the action is seen as if it were centered on a stage in a theater, and the spectator (the reader) keeps his or her eyes and ears closely glued to this one spot for all of the action and dialogue. For example, Hester on the scaffold in penance is the focal point for all eyes. The women in the crowd who criticize her so unkindly focus on her. The "stranger" eyes her curiously. Governor Bellingham, Reverend Wilson, and Reverend Dimmesdale all stare at her. Hester is a still figure around whom much activity takes place. (This type of character placement is often seen in the theater.) The whole first chapter is a dramatic buildup to Hester's entrance in Chapter II. Near the end of Chapter III, after Dimmesdale has asked Hester to name her lover, he delivers a dramatic "aside," lines spoken privately by an actor and supposed to be heard by the audience but not by the other actors. She has refused to identify Pearl's father, and the relieved minister murmurs aloud, "She will not speak! Wondrous strength and generosity of a woman's heart! She will not speak!" The "audience"—in this case, the reader—receives the full impact of this revealing dramatic statement, but the "other actors"—the officials on the balcony and the crowd below—do not hear it.

INTRODUCTION
"THE CUSTOM HOUSE"

Hawthorne wrote a long introductory sketch for *The Scarlet Letter* titled "The Custom House." The sketch may be divided into six sections: (1) the introduction and a description of the Salem Custom House; (2) a discussion of Hawthorne's Salem ancestry; (3) character sketches of three officials with whom Hawthorne serves in the Salem Custom House; (4) Surveyor Pue's manuscript; (5) Hawthorne's theory of romance; and (6) various comments concerning Hawthorne's loss of his position in the Salem Custom House. Hawthorne begins his sketch by mentioning that he has an "autobiographical impulse." He wishes to have a "talk" with the reader. He indicates that his "main purpose" is to picture a way of life in the Salem Custom House not before described. He also wishes to describe "some of the characters that move" in the Custom House circle (including himself, of course). The Salem Custom House is seen as a large, roomy brick building with a huge figure of the American eagle over the front door. Grass grows in the chinks between the pavements, for Salem has begun to decline as Boston and New York become important port cities. The big, cobwebbed main office is near the front door, which overlooks the wharf. Hawthorne discusses his "feeling for old Salem," a sensation he calls "affection." He remembers that his own ancestors arrived in Salem about two hundred and twenty-five years before this time. He recollects his "first ancestor" in America, a stately Puritan with Bible and sword, a man who later as a judge harshly persecuted the Quakers. The son of this soldier-judge was well known for his part in the Salem witchcraft trials. Jumping to the present time, Hawthorne offers an apology for himself, because he is a mere "writer of storybooks." However, he explains in great detail that he has always felt it his "destiny" to make Salem his home. Consequently, he has been very pleased to accept an appointment in the Salem Custom House as "chief executive officer" (surveyor of the revenue). Then begin three long descriptions of Hawthorne's fellow workers in the customs service. The first picture is of the "Oldest Inhabitant," the collector named General Miller—"New England's most distinguished soldier" and a man of habit who is described as "radically conservative." Most of the "wearisome old souls" Hawthorne works with are elderly, retired sea captains. The old men "peep into the holds of vessels," fussing about unimportant trifles while matters of real importance are often ignored. Hawthorne claims that he grows to like them all. He pictures them in the back entry of the building with their chairs tilted against the wall, joyfully exchanging stale jokes. The next detailed description is of the "father of the Custom House—the patriarch," the oldest member of the group. He is a "permanent Inspector." About eighty years old, this official has little intellect, wonderful fine physical health, and a very small amount of the moral and spiritual virtues. Hawthorne emphasizes this picture by declaring that this man has "no soul, no heart, no mind; nothing . . . but instincts." The inspector's greatest joy is "to recollect the good dinners" that he has eaten during a long lifetime. Next, Hawthorne goes back to his description of the Collector. About seventy years old, this aged gentleman can barely make his way up the steps of the Custom House. Then he spends his time quietly sitting in his chair by the fireplace, radiating a "mild and kindly" look. The next character description is of an unnamed "man of business," who is a great contrast to the inefficient, nonworking officials of the Salem Custom House. This "prompt, acute, clear-minded" customs officer is the "mainspring" that keeps all the Custom House "wheels in motion." He is honest, intelligent, and regular in the administration of business affairs

The next part of the sketch is devoted to a description of a large, unfinished chamber above the collector's rooms where Hawthorne pokes around in a pile of old documents to discover a "small package, carefully done up in a piece of ancient parchment." The package was once the property of Surveyor Jonathan Pue, who served the Salem Custom House about 1750, a hundred years before Hawthorne's tour of duty. The documents are of a private nature and are written out in Surveyor Pue's own handwriting. In the "mysterious package" is a "worn and faded" piece of "fine red cloth" with torn "gold embroidery" around it. It is in the shape of the capital letter *A*, with each limb of the letter being "three inches and a quarter in length." Hawthorne carefully inspects the strange letter. Then he casually places it on his breast. With a shudder, he drops it, for he feels a horrifying sensation of "burning heat . . . as if the letter were not of red cloth, but red-hot iron." Suddenly, Hawthorne notices that the red cloth letter is accompanied by explanatory documents, written up by Surveyor Pue. The papers are a record of the life and conversation of a woman named Hester Prynne who lived in Boston during the middle and late years of the seventeenth century. The contents of these records form the main basis of *The Scarlet Letter*. The next major section of "The Custom House" is devoted to a description of Hawthorne's own theory of romance; that is, an account of some of the physical conditions necessary for him to be able to write the sort of long tale he calls a romance. The last part of "The Custom House" is about Hawthorne's dismissal from his post. He describes himself as becoming "melancholy and restless" in the customs service. He wonders how much longer he can "stay in the Custom House, and yet go forth a man." During his third year as surveyor, the Whig candidate, General Zachary Taylor, is elected to the presidency. Hawthorne is of another political party, a Democrat. He loses his position, according to the long-established custom of the spoils system. With the suggestion that "Providence" (the wisdom of God) has helped end his bored existence in the Salem Custom House, Hawthorne makes "an investment in ink, paper, and steel-pens" and again becomes "a literary man."

COMMENT

When Hawthorne writes "The Custom House," he is in the process of recovering from a great deal of resentment caused by the loss of his job. Although he explains in much detail how very glad he is to be free of his boring work, there is a bit of sour grapes in his attitude about the whole affair. He writes in the sketch that "Uncle Sam claims as his share" only "three hours and a half" each day. There is relatively little for him to do. His pay is quite satisfactory. It is no small wonder that he should protest. He feels that he has done his work well. He resents being removed. He also is disturbed at the poor quality of customs officers, in general. Thus, his bitter—almost cruel—portrait of the Inspector helps express his annoyance. Hawthorne seems enraged when he writes that customs officials are appointed to serve "their own profit and convenience" and that they are seldom chosen with any "reference to their fitness for the duty to be performed." Many people in Salem are very upset with Hawthorne because he writes so acidly of his native town. He is perhaps aware that in writing this sketch he is penning a farewell to Salem, the home of his ancestors. He declares that, from this time on, Salem "ceases to be a reality" of his life. He is a "citizen of somewhere else." For much of the rest of his residence in America, he lives in Concord.

THE SCARLET LETTER
SUMMARY

Hester Prynne has shocked the Puritans of Boston by committing adultery. Two years before the opening of the story, she was sent to America alone by her husband to await his arrival. As far as the world knows, Hester's husband, Dr. Prynne (an elderly scientist), has disappeared. All of Boston is anxious for Hester to tell the name of her secret lover, the father of her child named Pearl. Hester leaves the prison and walks to the marketplace where she mounts the steps of a scaffold. The magistrates have been merciful to her—she has not been condemned to death for her crime against society. However, she is to stand on the scaffold for several hours so that the townspeople may see her, the tiny three-month-old baby, and the cloth scarlet letter *A* she wears on her bosom. Governor Bellingham, the Reverend John Wilson, and the Reverend Arthur Dimmesdale try to get Hester to name her lover. She refuses, much to the relief of Dimmesdale. While Hester is trying to forget the horror of the present (by remembering the past), she sees a familiar figure on the edge of the crowd. This "stranger" is her husband, Dr. Prynne, who cautions her (by placing a finger to his lips) against recognizing him publicly. Later, in the prison, Dr. Prynne (under the newly assumed name of Roger Chillingworth) comes to see Hester and demands to know the name of Hester's lover. She refuses to tell him. He then forces her to take an oath that she will not admit to anyone that he is her husband.

Soon Hester leaves the prison and takes up residence in a small cottage by the seashore. She earns her living by fine sewing and embroidering, especially on elaborate garments for the magistrates (judges) to wear on special occasions. Hester's child, Pearl, grows into a beautiful child, but she will not be managed easily. Sometimes her mother is upset at the "freakish, elfish" look that comes into Pearl's eyes. Hester goes to Governor Bellingham's mansion to see him, for she understands that he, among others, feels that Pearl should be taken from her. While they are waiting for the governor to appear, Pearl is highly amused to see her mother's scarlet letter *A* reflected in the brightly polished metal surface of the breastplate of a suit of armor. Governor Bellingham soon appears and, aided by Reverend Wilson, questions Pearl about her religious education. The response is so unsatisfactory to the governor that he feels sure that Pearl should leave her mother. Then Hester appeals to Dimmesdale who is standing nearby. He convinces Governor Bellingham that it would be best for all if Hester and Pearl remained together. Roger Chillingworth, suspicious of Arthur Dimmesdale, becomes his medical attendant and constant companion. Eventually, the two men live in the same house.

Chillingworth, in general terms, baits Dimmesdale, discussing the value of confession in relieving the burden of a guilty soul. Dimmesdale answers him in general terms about confession. He explains why he believes some people dare not confess: they are afraid that they will lose their good reputations and will then have no further opportunity to serve mankind. He and Chillingworth part, almost in a quarrel. Later, Chillingworth walks into the chamber of the sleeping Dimmesdale and lifts away the upper part of his garment to reveal a horrifying sight on Dimmesdale's breast. Dimmesdale punishes himself by long night watches, sometimes whipping himself, at other times fasting or praying for long hours. Once in a while he studies his face reflected in a mirror.

One night he feels that he can stand this no longer. He goes out into the marketplace and mounts the steps of the scaffold where Hester once stood in penance. He shrieks aloud, but no one hears him but Governor Bellingham and his sister, Mistress Hibbins, who peer out their windows and then quickly go back to bed. Soon, Hester and Pearl walk by, on their way home from the bedside of the dying Governor Winthrop. At Dimmesdale's request, the two join him on the scaffold, and the three join hands there. Chillingworth soon appears and, after a meteor has lighted up the landscape, leads Dimmesdale home. Hester is surprised at the weak state of health in which she finds Dimmesdale. She knows that Chillingworth has been subtly torturing him, so she resolves to seek out the old physician to see if she can aid the unhappy minister. She talks with Chillingworth and ends up saying that she "must reveal the secret": that is, explain that the old physician is her husband. Learning that Dimmesdale has journeyed into the forest to see the Apostle Eliot "among his Indian converts," Hester waits for the visiting minister in the forest. Pearl plays nearby in the sunshine, which always disappears when Hester approaches. Dimmesdale arrives with his hand over his heart—a familiar gesture of his. Hester tells Arthur Dimmesdale that his "friend" Chillingworth is his enemy. He is disturbed at the news. Then he and Hester make plans to escape the colony with Pearl. Hester removes her scarlet letter and lets down her long hair from under a tight cap. They invite Pearl to join them, but the child will not approach until Hester replaces the scarlet letter on her breast. The plans for the escape are completed. They will leave on Monday, the day after Arthur Dimmesdale delivers the Election Sermon (a great honor to any Boston minister). On the way home from the forest, Dimmesdale (temporarily relieved from pangs of conscience and remorse) meets, and is tempted to say evil words to, the following people: one of the elderly deacons of his church; the oldest "female member" of his congregation; the newest and youngest feminine member of his church; a group of little Puritan children; a member of the "ship's crew from the Spanish Main"; and Mistress Hibbins. He resists the temptation to shock or surprise them. He arrives home, eats a good meal, and spends all night writing his Election Sermon.

On the day of the New England Holiday set aside to celebrate the annual election of the chief magistrate, there is a procession made up of musicians, soldiers, the leading magistrates, and the speaker of the day—the Reverend Arthur Dimmesdale.

The minister seems full of energy. He does not know that the ship captain has just informed Hester that Chillingworth will be one of the traveling party on board the ship bound for Bristol, England. Hester faintly hears Dimmesdale's sermon as she stands near the scaffold. He thrills his audience with his expressive oratory. When the crowd is in the marketplace, it loudly cheers him. As the procession forms again and starts to leave the marketplace, Dimmesdale is seen to be weakly tottering. Refusing all help, he stops when his part of the procession nears the scaffold. He calls Hester and Pearl to him, and with Hester's help he climbs the scaffold steps. (Chillingworth tries to stop him.) Then Arthur Dimmesdale confesses that he is Pearl's father, after which he reveals the "red stigma" on his breast. After this, he dies on the scaffold.

The story concludes with people's differing reports of what they heard and saw in the marketplace on the scaffold. Chillingworth loses his purpose (of vengeance) in life, and he dies within the year, leaving much property in England and America to Pearl. Soon, Hester and Pearl leave Boston and disappear. Later, Hester returns alone, and again taking up the scarlet letter *A*, she lives alone in the same small cottage by the seashore. It is thought that Pearl is happily married in Europe. After a long, full life of giving advice to women who are troubled by affairs of the heart, Hester dies and is buried beside Arthur Dimmesdale.

THE SCARLET LETTER
CHAPTERS I–IV

CHAPTER I: "THE PRISON-DOOR"

Hester Prynne has committed adultery. Two years ago her husband in Europe sent her on ahead to America while he settled some business affairs. Alone in the small town of Boston, Hester has shocked and angered her neighbors by secretly taking a lover and bringing forth a child. The Puritans of Boston are shocked that she has done this thing. They are angry because she will not reveal the name of the father of the child. Although the usual penalty for adultery is death, the Puritan judges (called magistrates) have decided to be merciful to her, declaring that Hester's punishment will be to stand for several hours on the scaffold (a high platform near the marketplace) in full view of everyone. She will hold her infant in her arms and will be wearing on the breast of her dress a piece of scarlet cloth formed into the letter *A*. She will continue to wear this letter on her breast for the rest of her life.

As the story opens in the month of June 1642, a group of Puritan men and women gather in front of the door of the prison waiting for Hester to make her appearance. The early settlers felt it necessary to build a prison and to set aside a cemetery as stern reminders of life and death. The gloomy building looks out on a grass plot covered with "unsightly vegetation" except for one wild rosebush that blossoms near the threshold of the prison. The "fragrance and fragile beauty" of this one simple flower is a "token" (a symbol) that Nature may pity us, even though we may be inhuman to one another. The author wonders about the origin of the rosebush—whether it has perhaps survived the wilderness in which it originally grew, or whether it had "sprung up" in the footsteps of another rebellious woman, who, a few years before, had entered the same prison door. At the "threshold" of the story, the author picks one of the roses and presents it to the reader "to symbolize" the "moral blossom" (in other words, the happy ending) of this tale of human weakness and sorrow.

COMMENT

The first sentence of the romance introduces a major character; that is, the community. The predominant mood of the tale is established by the words "sad-colored" and "gray." The word "hoods" suggests the secrecy and hypocrisy of a leading male character, Arthur Dimmesdale; in contrast, "bareheaded" represents the open repentance of Hester, the main female character, who wears the scarlet letter. The setting is Puritan Boston, near the present site of King's Chapel on Tremont Street. Following the literary principle of "associational psychology" (which connects certain places and historic scenes with current problems and tensions of characters), the introduction of the words "Boston," "Cornhill," "King's Chapel," and "Ann Hutchinson" brings to the mind of the reader a picture of historic Boston and early American Puritanism. The title *The Scarlet Letter* has a symbolic word in it. Thus it is suitable that the first chapter should refer to a symbol (a "token"), the red blossom of the "wild rose-bush." Whereas the scarlet letter is the symbol of Hester's adultery (the reason why she is wearing the letter *A* on her breast), the rosebush is symbolic of the sympathetic heart of nature, contrasted with the "unsightly vegetation" of the prison yard, which represents the hard-hearted Puritans about to stare at and denounce Hester. (She is to stand on a high platform, called a scaffold, in full view of everyone, as a public penance for committing adultery.) Near the end of the chapter, the mention of the name "Ann Hutchinson" is very interesting, for she was an early fighter for women's rights. Hester Prynne, later on in the story, is in her own way a sort of feminist. There is, in the same sentence mentioning Ann Hutchinson, a fine example of

Hawthorne's use of the indirect method. Using the word "whether" several times in a row, he presents a number of possibilities as to what the answer to a question might be. He allows the thinking reader to make up his or her own mind about the suitable answer to the question. The theatrical technique of indicating that the reader is at the "threshold" of the tale (in this instance, Hester's prison door sill) is a typical Hawthorne device. (This same idea is used at the beginning of *The House of the Seven Gables,* the romance that follows *The Scarlet Letter.*)

CHAPTER II: "THE MARKET-PLACE"

The scene begins in front of the jail in Prison Lane. The Puritans of Boston stare at the door that Hester Prynne will come through. The author mentions the people who may possibly come out of the prison door on the way to punishment in the marketplace. Perhaps a "sluggish bond servant" or an "undutiful child" is to be whipped. Perhaps one of another religious group (or even an Indian) is to be driven out of town. Perhaps there is to be death at the gallows for a witch, like Mistress Hibbins, Governor Bellingham's sister. Little sympathy is given anyone on the way to the town scaffold. The watchers are very solemn, which is suitable for people for whom religion and law mean practically the same thing. From a group of five women comes the first dialogue in the story. One "hard-featured dame of fifty" feels that Hester Prynne's sentence is much too slight. Another joins in to suggest that the Reverend Arthur Dimmesdale, Hester's minister, is disturbed at the "scandal" in his congregation. A third adds that she believes the magistrates (the judges) should brand Hester's forehead, for she suspects the guilty woman capable of covering up the scarlet letter on her breast with a pin. A fourth woman, a young mother, gently remarks that Hester might cover up the letter, but the pain of it will remain "always in her heart." The fifth and most cruel of these self-appointed "judges" strongly declares that the laws of both the

Bible and the colony demand Hester's death for adultery. A nearby man finds fault with the small group of women; he points out that the door of the prison is about to be opened.

First, there appears an official whose appearance suggests the "whole dismal severity of the Puritanic code of law." He pulls along Hester Prynne, who bears in her arms little Pearl, an infant about three months old. (Even at this moment when she comes through the prison door, Hester walks with "natural dignity and force of character." This emphasizes her independent spirit.) Blinking, the infant tries to turn its face away from the strong sun. At first, Hester wants to cover her scarlet letter by holding the baby close to her bosom. Deciding that "one token of her shame" (the child) will "poorly serve to hide another" (the scarlet letter), she places the child on her arm and looks around at the townspeople. For the first time, the observers get a good look at Hester's symbol of adultery. It is the letter *A* on "fine red cloth, surrounded with an elaborate embroidery and fantastic flourishes of gold thread," attached to the bodice of her gown. Hester is a woman of large build with an elegant figure. She has very glossy, "dark and abundant hair," a beautiful face with regular features, a rich complexion, and distinct brows and dark eyes. Her womanly qualities, emphasizing "state and dignity," shine even at the moment when she leaves the jail. Her dress, made when she was in the prison, appears to express the spirit and the "desperate recklessness of her mood." (She dares to express her independence only in the matter of her clothing.) The scarlet token awes the townspeople. Again, three of the women criticize Hester, this time pointing out her dress. The third of the trio asks for charity toward the fallen woman. The official announces that Hester is to show her letter on the scaffold in the marketplace until one hour past noon. Then he cries out a blessing that in the "righteous" Massachusetts Bay Colony sin is "dragged out into the sunshine."

Hester, followed by a crowd of "stern-browed men," "unkindlyvisaged women," and "curious schoolboys," begins the walk from the jail to the marketplace. Though her manner seems proud, she is in agony, as if her heart were being trampled on by the accusing Puritans. She finally arrives at a scaffold erected almost beneath the eaves of a church. This scaffold is the platform of a pillory (a device used to hold tightly a person's neck and wrists). Hester is not to be placed in this device but is to stand for a certain length of time on the platform (which is "about the height of a man's shoulder above the street"), displaying two tokens of her adultery—the scarlet letter and her child. A Papist (Roman Catholic) would perhaps be reminded of "the image of Divine Maternity" (the Virgin Mary) by this picture of Hester and her infant. However, the unhappy Puritan mother does not represent the "sacred image of sinless motherhood." On a balcony of the meeting house overlooking the pillory platform are seen standing the most important personages of the colony: the governor, several of his counselors, a judge, a general, and the ministers of the town.

To lessen her intense mental suffering, Hester's mind and memory turn back to her past in Europe, as she pictures "scenes" and faces much contrasted with the rough town streets and inhabitants of the Boston colony. She reviews happenings from her infancy as well as from her school days. Also, recollections of things of more recent years fly through her mind like events in a "play." Because she tries to lose herself in memories of the past, she is able to endure the humiliation of the moment. From the "point of view" of the scaffold, Hester summarizes the important places and people in her life since the days of her infancy. She visualizes her native village in Old England and her parents' poor home. She thinks again of her father and mother, recalling their love and concern for her welfare. She remembers her own youthful face. She examines a face, "well stricken in years, a pale, thin, scholar-like visage." Her reminiscence stays with this elderly scholar: she recalls that his eyes, dim and weary from reading books, once in a while would attempt to analyze the "human soul." She further pictures his figure, "slightly deformed, with the left shoulder a trifle higher than the right." Next, Hester's mind wanders to the scene of a continental European city to which she went as the wife of this "misshapen scholar." She in her youth was "like a tuft of green moss"; he in his old age resembled the "crumbling wall" to which she in her poverty-stricken "green" youth had to cling. Hester's mind then jumps ahead several years. She is rudely brought back to where she is on the scaffold. In amazement, she clutches the child to her breast and looks down. Then, having difficulty in believing that she is standing where she is, she places her finger on the scarlet letter.

COMMENT

The Puritans believed in a theocratic state where the church and state share authority. This is based on the social order pictured in the Old Testament, and it is explained by scholarly clergymen (such as John Wilson and Arthur Dimmesdale, English university graduates). Emphasis is placed on the biblical Covenant that promises obedience to elected leaders ("magistrates" in the Puritan colony) who may easily be replaced because of poor leadership. The Puritan theocracy, with the church and state having equal responsibility for keeping law and order in the colony, is always in the background of the story. It helps explain the different professions represented by the characters assembled on the balcony overlooking the scaffold (the governor, a military man, and the ministers). The Scriptures demand death for adultery, and the Puritan laws closely follow the biblical pattern. The Puritan "fathers" stress fidelity in marriage and the sacredness of the family. Thus, Hester's crime of adultery is punishable by death. Since her husband (Dr. Prynne) is reported to be dead, the magistrates extend to her what they consider to be "great mercy." Hester is a typical nineteenth-century woman of ill repute (as far as literature goes), for she has dark hair and is of a passionate nature. Hawthorne describes many of the scenes as if they were seen by a spectator from a theater seat; that is, as if the setting, the characters, and the action were all viewed on the picture frame stage of the movies or the theater. The "dusky mirror" is the first of Hawthorne's many shiny surfaces used for literary purposes in this story. In this case, Hester is rapidly reviewing her past life in the gloomy "mirror" of intro-spection; that is, she analyzes her own previous life before coming to Boston. (Most of the other mirrors in this book have physical surfaces; they are not reflections of the imagination. See below.) Hester remembers that the prying eyes of her husband, Dr. Prynne, were once capable of analyzing people. This is a subtle foreshadowing of the horrors to come later in the tale, when the scientist Chillingworth (actually Dr. Prynne) attempts in revenge to examine the soul of the guilty and hypocritical Dimmesdale.

CHAPTER III: "THE RECOGNITION"

Hester Prynne is observed on the scaffold by a man who recognizes her. The "stranger" learns her story from a towns-man. Reverend Wilson, Governor Bellingham, and Reverend Dimmesdale all speak to Hester, each concerned that she should tell the name of her lover. When Dimmesdale asks her and she refuses to tell, the minister is greatly relieved.

Hester sees an Indian at the edge of the crowd watching her. Beside him is the "figure" of a "white man, clad in a strange disarray of civilized and savage costume." He is short, has a wrinkled face, and reveals "a remarkable intelligence in his features." When she notes that one of his shoulders is higher than the other, she instinctively presses the infant to her bosom. At first, the "stranger" casually observes Hester. Suddenly, he recognizes her. Noting that Hester is staring at him, also in recognition, he deliberately raises his finger to his lips in a gesture of secrecy. Casually questioning a townsman in general terms as to Hester's identity and the nature of her crime, he responds to this information with an account of his own "grievous mishaps by sea and land," and of his being held in captivity by Indians in the south. He has been brought to Boston to be ransomed. The "stranger" is given a detailed description by the townsman of Hester Prynne's husband (whom the reader suspects to be the questioner himself). He finds himself pictured as a "learned man, English by birth," who, after living for a long time in Amsterdam, had decided to come to the New World to join the Massachusetts Bay Colony. Remaining in Holland to settle some "necessary affairs," he had sent his wife (Hester Prynne) ahead. Over a period of two years, nothing has been heard of him, and his wife has brought forth a child. Smiling bitterly, "the stranger" asks the name of the father of the child. He is told that "Madam Hester absolutely refuseth to speak" and that "the guilty one" may be watching her at this very moment. Because Hester is "youthful and fair," because she was probably "strongly tempted to her fall," and also because "her husband may be at the bottom of the sea," the magistrates have not given her the penalty of death. She has been sentenced to stand for "three hours on the platform of the pillory" and then, for the rest of her life, to wear on her bosom the scarlet letter *A*, signifying adultery or adulteress. Considering this a "wise sentence," the "stranger" regrets that the name is not known of the father of the child. Three times he says, "he will be known!" Then he leaves.

Hester has been almost overwhelmed at the sight of Roger Prynne and is glad to see him in the presence of the "thousand witnesses," rather than "to greet him, face to face, they two alone." She dreads the moment when the two of them will be together alone. All at once, she hears a voice behind her, coming from the balcony attached to the meeting house. She looks up to see Governor Bellingham, surrounded by four sergeants and some very dignified members of the

Puritan community. The speaker, "a man of kind and genial spirit," is the famous scholar John Wilson, the oldest clergyman in Boston. Familiar with "the shaded light of his study," he seems unsuitable to be one dealing "with a question of human guilt, passion, and anguish." He tells Hester that his youthful fellow clergyman, her own pastor (the Reverend Arthur Dimmesdale), should force her to tell the name of the father of the child. He explains Dimmesdale's point of view that it is "wronging the very nature of woman to force her to lay open her heart's secrets in such broad daylight, and in presence of so great a multitude." At this point, Governor Bellingham declares Dimmesdale responsible for obtaining Hester's "repentance" and "confession."

All eyes turn to observe the young minister. He has a "very striking aspect," with a high forehead, large, brown eyes, and a "tremulous" mouth. He has a "half-frightened look" and is evidently a person who likes to be alone. Reverend Wilson pleads with him to speak. Dimmesdale begins by looking steadily into her eyes and telling her that she must understand that he, as her pastor, is accountable for her behavior. If she feels that for her "soul's peace" she should confess the name of her "fellow-sinner and fellow-sufferer," then she should "speak out the name." Her sin has been revealed, and she will "work out an open triumph over the evil" within her. But, he continues, the father of the child may not have the "courage" to confess and must therefore "add hypocrisy to sin." All of the listeners think the young minister's touching speech will cause Hester to confess. Even the infant looks toward the speaker. But Hester will not speak the name. Reverend Wilson suggests that confession would help remove the scarlet letter from her bosom. Hester refuses again, saying that she wishes she might endure the "agony" of the father of the child. A cold and stern voice from the crowd (Dr. Prynne's voice) demands that she speak. Again she refuses. Arthur Dimmesdale, in a dramatic aside, murmurs: "She will not speak!" Then, for over an hour, Reverend Wilson speaks to

the crowd about various kinds of sin, making many references to the scarlet letter on Hester's breast. Exhausted, Hester
stands on the scaffold, occasionally and mechanically attempting to hush the wails and screams of the infant in her arms.
Finally, she is returned to the darkness of the prison.

COMMENT

Note that over and over again, both in the dialogue and
in Hawthorne's descriptive passages, the white man who
stands on the edge of the crowd is called the "stranger."
This is Hawthorne's bow to a literary convention of his
day, the introduction of an "unknown" character, often
called the "stranger." (Both Hawthorne and his literary
contemporary, James Fenimore Cooper, borrow this
artistic device from the English novelist Sir Walter Scott.)
Each of Hawthorne's romances features an "unknown"
character. It is ironical that the "stranger" (actually Dr.
Prynne in disguise) must hear his own story retold by a
townsman, but this is a fine device for allowing the reader
to gain more knowledge of Hester's past. The placing of
the clergy and the magistrates together on the balcony
points to the fact that in a theocracy (a state ruled by
God), the state is the arm of the church, charged with
enforcing its edicts. Reverend Wilson's comments about
his fellow clergyman, Dimmesdale, allow the reader to
have a good picture in his mind of the young minister
before he speaks. (Compare the effect of this speech by
Dimmesdale with that of his Election Day Sermon in
Chapter XXII.) Dimmesdale describes how he feels about
his own involvement in Hester's sin, but the members
of the audience, of course, do not realize that he is telling of his own suffering. When he urges Hester to speak
and she still refuses, the young clergyman murmurs an
"aside": "Wondrous strength and generosity of a woman's
heart! She will not speak!" An aside is lines spoken
privately by an actor and supposed to be heard only by
the audience. This use of the aside shows the influence

of the theater on Hawthorne, as well as his use of melo-dramatic, Gothic writing techniques of his own day, emphasizing artificial, theatrical devices.

CHAPTER IV: "THE INTERVIEW"

Hester and her baby, Pearl, both need medical attention, so a physician named Roger Chillingworth is brought to them in the prison. He is the "stranger" (actually, Dr. Prynne, her husband). After giving them medical care, Chillingworth discusses Hester's situation, demanding to know the name of her lover. She refuses to tell him. Back in the prison, Hester Prynne is found to be "in a state of nervous excitement," so much so that the jailer, Master Brackett, thinks it best to bring in a doctor. The infant also seems to be in deep distress. Master Brackett brings into Hester's cell "the stranger" who earlier that day was so very much interested in her case. (For the purpose of convenience, he is living in the prison until his ransom has been arranged with the Indians.) The physician is introduced as Roger Chillingworth. He asks to see Hester alone, claiming that he will cause her to be more ready to accept "just authority" than she has been thus far. First, he cares for the child, by preparing some simple remedy. Hester thinks he wishes to poison the baby, but he assures her that the medicine will be good for it. Shortly, the infant sleeps. After looking intently for a while at Hester, he mixes a drink to help calm her. She questions him as to whether or not the medicine will kill her. He explains that he wishes for her to live, so that the "burning shame" (the scarlet letter) will continue to "blaze" upon her bosom. At this point, he touches the letter, and it seems to "scorch into Hester's breast," as if it were "red-hot." She drinks the medicine and seats herself on the bed, with him in a chair beside her.

He begins to talk, blaming himself for marrying a girl of her youth and beauty. He says that he should have known from the beginning that she would someday be wearing a scarlet letter. Hester quietly replies, "I was frank with thee. I felt no love." He admits that she had not deceived him in this respect. He remarks that his life had been lonely and "cheerless" before he had married her. She had brought "warmth" into his existence. At this time, Hester murmurs that she has "wronged" him. He answers that they "have wronged each other" and that his was "the first wrong" because he, an old man, should never have married a "budding youth." Thus, Chillingworth says, "I seek no vengeance, plot no evil against thee. Between thee and me, the scale hangs fairly balanced." Then he demands to know the name of Hester's lover. She replies, "Ask me not! That thou shalt never know!" He tells her that few things remain "hidden from the man, who devotes himself" to the "solution of a mystery." All others may be deceived as to the man's name, but he will not be. He declares, "I shall seek this man." He feels that he will find him, for there will exist a certain bond of sympathy between the lover and himself when he comes near him. Hester's lover will "tremble," and Chillingworth will "shudder" in response. Then, Hester's husband cries out, "Sooner or later, he must needs be mine!" Chillingworth realizes that Hester's lover will wear "no letter of infamy wrought into his garment," but he claims he will be able to read the letter on the guilty man's heart. He will not betray him to the law, threaten his life, or even damage his reputation. Also, the unknown lover may even "hide himself in outward honor."

Chillingworth then asks Hester to do but one thing, to keep secret the fact that he is Dr. Prynne, her husband. Even though she is not to be known as his wife, he still feels a closeness of connection with her and intends to stay in the town where she, her child, and her lover live. Hester asks why he does not publicly reveal her identity as his wife and cast her off. He explains that it might be that he does not care to be known as the husband of a "faithless woman." Then Hester swears an oath that as far as the rest of the world is concerned her husband (Dr. Prynne) is dead. Above all, she is not to tell the secret of her husband's identity to her lover. Chillingworth smiles as he leaves Hester. She asks if he is "like the Black Man that haunts the forest." She wonders if he has led her into a "bond that will prove the ruin" of her soul. He says, "Not thy soul. No, not thine!" Thus Chillingworth's cold and devilish revenge begins.

COMMENT

Throughout the romance, Pearl is seen as a token, a living representation, of her mother's sin of adultery. In this chapter the child's "convulsions of pain" physically parallel the "moral agony" endured that day by the unhappy mother. When the doctor, Roger Chillingworth, prepares to soothe the child by some medicine, Hester is afraid that he wishes to kill her; but he has no such object in mind. When Hester asks him whether he is giving her a poisonous drink, he explains to her that he does not desire her death, for he wishes her to live, and seeks "no vengeance" against her. But he establishes here the point that he does seek revenge on Hester's lover. Thus, one of the main threads of the plot begins here: Chillingworth's search for, and revenge on, the father of Pearl. He indicates that he intends to "ruin" the soul of his victim. Often, Hawthorne tells us about his characters through elaborate descriptions of their actions and thoughts. Note that in this chapter the intimate conversation between Hester and her husband reveals much about their past actions and helps us anticipate their future patterns of action.

THE SCARLET LETTER
CHAPTERS V–IX

CHAPTER V: "HESTER AT HER NEEDLE"

Hester tries to accustom herself to the "daily custom" of always being "the general symbol at which the preacher and moralist might point." She knows that pure, young people will "be taught to look at her . . . as the figure, the body, the reality of sin." She has nothing to look forward to but an endless series of burdensome days, "each its own trial." She is not restricted by the judgment handed down to her by the magistrates to stay in Boston. She may leave and return to Europe; it would even be possible to disappear into the forest and live among the Indians. But she seems compelled to stay in the place where a "great and marked event has given . . . color" to her life. Her "sin" is the root "she had struck into the soil." She is held by a "chain" made "of iron links." It is possible that she stays in Boston because her former lover is near her. She tells herself that "the scene of her guilt" has been here, and "the torture of her daily shame" will eventually cleanse her soul.

Hester settles herself and her infant child on the edge of the town in a small, abandoned, thatched cottage, not near any other settler's home. Her "lonesome dwelling" is near the sea. People begin to look at her house with questioning eyes. Small children find their way there and peep through the window to watch her sew. They might observe her standing in the doorway of her house, working in her garden, or walking along the path from town. Catching sight of the scarlet letter, they fearfully run away. Meanwhile, Hester earns her living by sewing. The "curiously embroidered letter" on her breast is a "specimen of her delicate and imaginative skill." Although most of the Puritans are required to wear dark and simple clothing, for public ceremonies (such as "the installation of magistrates") the officials wear "ruffs, painfully wrought bands, and gorgeously embroidered gloves." At funerals, both corpses and mourners are elaborately dressed. Baby linen is also very decorative. Hester's "handiwork" becomes "the fashion," for a variety of reasons, such as pity or curiosity. Possibly she sews better than anyone else at the time. At any rate, she is satisfactorily paid for as much sewing as she cares to do. Prominent people in Boston choose to wear the garments she makes. She sews the ruffs of the governor, military men's scarves, the minister's high collar, little caps for babies, and coffin clothes for the dead. The one thing she does not embroider is "the white veil . . . of a bride." This shows that "society" still frowns "upon her sin." For her labor, Hester asks in payment only enough for the simple needs of life for herself and some extras for Pearl. She dresses herself in dark, coarse material, which causes the scarlet letter to blaze out at the world in contrast. Pearl's dresses are seen to be "fanciful," accenting the "airy charm" of the child. The rest of her money Hester spends on charity, which is not always appreciated. She spends much time "making coarse garments for the poor."

Hester's "taste for the gorgeously beautiful" finds expression in "the delicate toil of the needle." She feels separated from society, even from those for whom she sews. Criticized severely at times by women "of elevated rank" and by the "poor" whom she often aids, Hester remains a patient martyr. One thing she will not do: she will not pray for her enemies, for she is fearful that "the words of the blessing" might "twist themselves into a curse."

Day after day, Hester suffers as a result of her sin. Ministers attract crowds in the street by giving her words of moral advice and choose her as the subject of sermons. Children run after her, condemning her with a fearful name. Strangers curiously regard the letter. And yet Hester never covers the token of her adultery with her hand, as she is sorely tempted to do at times. Once in a while someone (very likely Dimmesdale) looks at the letter, and for a moment she feels relief, "as if half of her agony" is being shared. Since Hester is alone much of the time, her "imagination" is "somewhat affected." She begins to believe that the scarlet letter has furnished her "with a new sense": that is, it gives her a "sympathetic knowledge of the hidden sin in other hearts." Her instinct tells her that "if truth were everywhere to be shown, a scarlet letter would blaze forth on many a bosom beside Hester Prynne's." Sometimes, she senses an "evil thing . . . at hand" when she passes a highly respected "minister or magistrate, the model of piety and justice." She feels a bond of "sisterhood" as she catches the "sanctified frown of some matron" of the highest reputation. At times, she is aware that a "companion" in sin is near her; looking up, she notes the eyes of a young maiden quickly withdrawn from the scarlet token of adultery. And yet, in the face of all these instances, Hester continues "to believe that no fellow-mortal" is "guilty like herself." Some idle gossips declare that the letter is not made of scarlet cloth, but that it is "red-hot with infernal fire," lighting Hester Prynne's path at nighttime.

COMMENT

This chapter fills in necessary background to the romance, beginning with the time when Hester comes from the prison to start life all over again, and continues through the first years of Pearl's existence. Deciding not to leave the colony, Hester finds a small cottage, physically isolated from the other members of the community, as she is spiritually separated from them. She earns her daily bread by expert sewing and embroidering of magnificent garments for public ceremonies. Of course, public prejudice does not allow her to make the white veil of a bride. Note that Hester, dressed in humble and somber clothes, must create for others beautiful clothing representative of worldly pomp and splendor. Hester begins the first of her many and continuing acts of charity toward others, some of whom only cruelly insult her, reminding her of her past sin. (Compare this with the ending of Chapter XXIV, where her *A* becomes a symbol for "Angel" because of her repeated good works.) Hester's experience with sin has made her able to recognize sin in others in Boston.

CHAPTER VI: "PEARL"

The infant Pearl, "a lovely and immortal flower," has sprung from "a guilty passion." As the child grows, the mother sees intelligence and beauty before her. Hester has named her baby Pearl because she represents a purchase of "great price." Humanity has given Hester a scarlet letter to remove her from "human sympathy," whereas God has given her a "lovely child," placed "on that same dishonored bosom." Hester is apprehensive that her own sin will be reflected in the child's nature by some "dark and wild peculiarity."

Pearl has "no physical defect," having "perfect shape," "vigor," and easy use of all her limbs. Her "native grace" and beauty are beautifully dressed by Hester in the "richest" cloth sold in Boston. The child's manner varies from that of a "peasant-baby" to that of "an infant princess." And yet with it all, she has her mother's passionate nature. She does not find it easy to obey rules. Hester recognizes in Pearl her own "wild, desperate, defiant mood, the flightiness of her temper," as well as the gloom that broods in her own heart. As to disciplining the child, Hester is not oversevere with her. At first, she tries to have a "tender, but strict control" over her, but eventually she finds out that both "smiles and frowns" prove of little help. Hester allows "the child to be swayed by her own impulses," according to the "caprice" of the moment. Sometimes the mother wonders if instead of a "human child" Pearl might be "an airy sprite," a creature from another world. In her "wild, bright, deeply-black eyes," there is a strange otherworldly look. Disturbed by the behavior of her unusual child, Hester sometimes bursts into "passionate tears." Pearl responds by frowns and an unsympathetic "look of discontent," or else she breaks out into "a rage of grief" as she tells her mother how much she loves her. Hester's "only real comfort" is when Pearl is asleep.

Soon the child grows old enough to talk with others, but she speaks to none but her mother, who is never without her on her walks about the town. Pearl sees other children, but she will not answer their greetings. If they group around her, she gathers up stones to throw at them and cries out in shrill tones. The "little Puritans" are very "intolerant" of the mother and child and often "scorn" them in their hearts and say unkind things to them. Both Hester and Pearl stand "together in the same circle of seclusion from human society." At home, the child makes companions of everyday objects. She talks with ancient pine trees, imagining them to be "Puritan elders." She sees the "ugliest weeds of the garden" as their children, and she steps on them or uproots them. Her rapid, darting activity resembles the "play of the northern lights." Among all of the varied "offspring of her own heart and mind," she never once creates a friend. Always she recognizes and attacks a world that is against her. Sometimes, Hester groans out, "What is this being which I have brought into the world!" Pearl answers only with a smile.

The "first object" of which Pearl seems to become aware is Hester's scarlet letter. When she is only an infant in the cradle, she reaches up her little hand and grasps it, attracted by "the glimmering of the gold embroidery about the letter." Gasping, Hester clutches the "token," and Pearl looks into her mother's eyes and smiles. After this time, Hester dreads when the child will look at the letter "with that peculiar smile" and the "odd expression of the eyes." Once, Hester looks at herself in "the small black mirror of Pearl's eyes," and she sees another face look out at her, "a face, fiend-like, full of smiling malice." On another day, Pearl picks "handfuls of wild-flowers" and throws them one by one at her mother's bosom. When she hits the scarlet letter, she excitedly dances up and down, much to the pain of her mother. Having thrown all of the flowers, she stands still and gazes at Hester. The mother imagines that a "little, laughing image of a fiend" is peeping out at her. Hester tells the child that their "Heavenly Father" sent her to earth.

Pearl positively answers, "I have no Heavenly Father!" Hester then recalls "the talk of the neighboring townspeople" that suggests that little Pearl is the "offspring" of a devil.

COMMENT

Pearl represents to Hester great sorrow (her adultery) and great joy (her child). Although the mother is not permitted to clothe herself in bright colors, she finds a sense of relief in dressing her child in gleaming colors, imaginatively arranged. Even as Hester's somber garments represent her restraint in dealing with the world around her, so, too, do Pearl's clothes reflect the child's spirited attitude toward everything about her. The unkind behavior of the Puritan children toward Pearl is parallel to the conduct of their parents toward Hester. Pearl has an aggressive attitude toward her mother, as well as her make-believe playmates and other children. She pains her mother by throwing flowers at the scarlet letter. Then she further disturbs Hester by asking where she (Pearl) came from. She rejects her mother's answer— her "Heavenly Father." This causes Hester to remember the talk of the townspeople regarding a theory that Pearl is descended from the devil. (This might be compared later on with Mistress Hibbins's attempts to connect Hester and Dimmesdale with the "Black Man of the Forest.")

CHAPTER VII: "THE GOVERNOR'S HALL"

One day Hester goes to Governor Bellingham's mansion to deliver a pair of "fringed and embroidered" gloves for him to wear on "some great occasion of state." At the moment, Governor Bellingham is not the chief magistrate of the colony, yet he is influential. Besides delivering the gloves, Hester has another more important reason for her trip: some people of Boston suggest that, for the good of her soul, Pearl should be removed from her mother's care. Governor Bellingham himself is one of the important people promoting this idea. Hester is accompanied on her way to the governor's mansion by Pearl. Pearl is seen as a child of "rich and luxuriant beauty" with deep glowing eyes and dark "glossy brown" hair. There is "fire in her and throughout her." She is dressed in a crimson velvet gown highly embroidered with gold thread. She seems a token of Hester's adultery, as much as the scarlet letter that her mother is "doomed to wear upon her bosom." As they walk along, Puritan children observe them and decide to throw mud at them. To their surprise Pearl frowns, stamps her feet, shakes her hand in a threatening gesture, and rushes at them, screaming. They flee.

They soon arrive at Governor Bellingham's large wooden mansion house. The outside is covered "with a kind of stucco, in which fragments of broken glass were plentifully inter-mixed." Pearl, pleased with the house, dances up and down in admiration, demanding that the sunshine that reflects from the broken bits of glass be "stripped off its front, and given her to play with." Her mother explains that this is impossible. They are greeted at the door by one of the governor's bond servants, wearing the customary blue coat of serving men of the period. They are told the governor is busy with several ministers and a "leech" (doctor). Hester grandly says she will enter. The servant, misinterpreting the "glittering symbol" on her bosom as an elaborate status symbol, admits her. Hester and Pearl walk around the hall of the mansion and inspect it. They see a wide and high room with tall windows at one end. The chairs are large and elaborately carved according to the style of the Elizabethan Age. On a table stands a "large pewter tankard" with a tiny bit of ale left in it. A row of portraits hang on the wall. The people represented in the pictures look like the "ghosts, rather than the pictures" of actual people. Featured in the center of the hall is a suit of mail of contemporary era. There is a particularly well-burnished helmet and breast-plate—so highly polished, in fact, that they "glow with white radiance, and scatter an illumination everywhere about upon the floor." Pearl stands admiring "the polished mirror of the breastplate." To Hester's surprise, the child says, "Mother, I see you here. Look! Look!" Hester sees that the shining breastplate has formed a peculiarly effective "convex mirror" exaggerating whatever is in the middle of the mirror. As she stands directly in front of the mirror the scarlet letter becomes the most prominent feature of her appearance. She seems absolutely hidden behind it. To increase her mother's discomfort, Pearl points upward "at a similar picture in the headpiece" that also exaggerates the scarlet letter. Hester's agony is increased as she sees reflected in the mirror Pearl's "look of naughty merriment." She draws Pearl aside to look at the garden. They see that attempts to create a formal English garden have failed, for cabbages and pumpkins are evident "in plain sight." They see rosebushes and apple trees. Pearl begins to cry for a red rose. Her mother hushes her as she hears the voices of the governor and his guests approach them. Just before the governor appears, Pearl gives a childish scream, for her curiosity is aroused by the coming of the gentlemen.

COMMENT

Much of this chapter is concerned with how the Puritans react to Pearl, whose "rich and luxuriant beauty," splendidly dressed by her mother, reminds everyone of Hester's adultery. Actually, Hester has spent many hours building up this likeness between Pearl and the scarlet letter. Even small Puritan children reject Pearl, who is quite capable of frightening them by screaming and rushing at them. The governor's mansion, with the sunshine reflecting from the tiny fragments of glass stuck into the stucco on the outside, is greatly admired by Pearl. Sunshine always appeals to Pearl. She even considers it a plaything. (The sun always seems to disappear when Hester appears. As the story unfolds, notice how the sun shines near Pearl and then is blotted out by a cloud at any time that Hester comes on the scene.) The breastplate of the suit of armor is convex (rounded outward, like the exterior of a globe). Any object reflected in the highly polished surface of this mirrorlike breastplate will be exaggerated in the middle; in fact, the center part, being nearer to what is being reflected, will present a larger picture than that seen on the edge of the "mirror." (This is what happens in highly exaggerated carnival mirrors.) When Hester stands exactly in front of this "convex mirror," the scarlet *A* is greatly exaggerated. The unusual largeness of the *A* is what Pearl so very gleefully calls to her mother's attention. There are double images in the headpiece of the suit of armor: first, Hester's scarlet letter; second, Pearl's "look of naughty merriment." Thus, the two main symbols of the romance come together here.

CHAPTER VIII: "THE ELF-CHILD AND THE MINISTER"

Governor Bellingham appears, accompanied by three men— John Wilson, Arthur Dimmesdale, and Roger Chillingworth. The governor has been pointing out the beauties of his estate. He looks more stern than he actually is. He is accustomed to living in luxury. Even such a venerable minister as the Reverend John Wilson approves of "good and comfortable things." But, of course, Reverend Wilson must disapprove "of such transgressions as that of Hester Prynne." Arthur Dimmesdale appears ill. Arriving suddenly at the door of his mansion, the governor almost stumbles over Pearl. She reminds him of the "children of the Lord of Misrule," tiny, fantastically dressed children participating in masks at the court of King James I. Pearl identifies herself and her mother, and the governor speaks in an uncomplimentary manner of Hester as a "scarlet woman."

At this point, Governor Bellingham assumes an official air and sternly explains to Hester that Boston officials question whether Pearl should be left to the "guidance" of one who has "stumbled and fallen." Frantically, Hester replies that she is capable of teaching her child. She says that she has learned from her experience. At this time, Reverend Wilson questions Pearl in religious matters. Obstinately, Pearl closes her lips and opens them only to mumble odd assortments of words. Finally, she announces that she has "been plucked by her mother off the bush of wild roses, that grow by the prison-door." The governor is astonished and immediately declares that Pearl is "in the dark as to her soul, its present depravity, and future destiny!" With great excitement, Hester reacts, exclaiming that the child is her "happiness" as well as her "torture." She cries out, "Pearl keeps me here in life! Pearl punishes me too!" Reverend Wilson assures her that the child will be "well cared for." Hester firmly declares, "I will not give her up!" Impulsively, she turns to Reverend Dimmesdale, saying, "speak for me! . . . Look thou to it! I will not lose the child! Look to it!"

Reverend Dimmesdale gently begins to discuss what he calls the "awful sacredness in the relation between this mother and this child." He points out that the child reminds people of the scarlet letter that "sears" Hester's bosom. He furthers his argument by claiming that Hester needs Pearl as a reminder of her past sin in order to "preserve her from blacker depths of sin into which Satan" might still plan to plunge her. The governor is satisfied. The child will remain with its mother. Dimmesdale quietly withdraws to a nearby window. Pearl softly steals toward him and "taking his hand in the grasp of both her own" leans her cheek against it. The minister responds by placing his hand on the child's head and then after a brief hesitation kisses her brow. Roger Chillingworth, looking much uglier and even more misshapen than he was three years ago, suggests that an observer might "analyze" Pearl's "nature" and "give a shrewd guess" at her father. As Hester leaves the governor's mansion, his "bitter-tempered sister," Mistress Hibbins, invites Hester to join a "merry company" that meets in the forest this very night under the guidance of "the Black Man." Hester smilingly refuses, saying that if Pearl had been taken from her, she would very likely have been in the party.

COMMENT

Dimmesdale seems to be suffering from poor health. One reason might be that he labors long and hard at his religious duties, but another—more important—reason is probably that he is plagued by his conscience, the knowledge of his hypocrisy. This is the first time in the romance that he seems to have changed to any extent or to have developed as a character. Governor Bellingham's reference to the "court mask" of King James I's time suggests that the governor has known a more sophisticated life in the past than that which Boston provides for him at the moment. (The masks of the English court were highly elaborate affairs, with symbolic characters wearing fantastic costumes.) Pearl reminds the governor of his past days when he sees her bright dress. Hester sees that Chillingworth's features have changed; he seems much more like a devil than before. He reacts to Dimmesdale's plea for Hester with the words: "You speak, my friend, with a strange earnestness." Perhaps he is beginning to suspect that Dimmesdale is the man he is seeking. Mistress Hibbins, who speaks to Hester when she leaves the mansion, is a caricature character, one whose personality, speech, and dress are extremely exaggerated to produce an absurd effect.

CHAPTER IX: "THE LEECH"

Roger Chillingworth (the name we shall give to him from now on) came out of the wilderness as an elderly, travelworn man. When he found his wife on the scaffold, he decided he wanted no public connection with her. He further decided that his life had taken on a "new purpose." He was determined to take revenge on his wife's lover. He finds that establishing himself as a doctor (sometimes called a leech) is an easy thing to do since Boston has no trained physician at the moment. People are delighted to have him become a member of the colony, not only because of their need for him but also because their beloved Mr. Dimmesdale is beginning to show signs of failing health. The young minister, himself, claims that Providence might see fit to remove him "because of his . . . unworthiness." As he says this, he places his hand over his heart, first growing red and then white, as if he were in pain. (This is the first time that Dimmesdale is noticed placing his hand over his heart. This action takes place many times as the story unfolds.)

Chillingworth wanders about the edges of the settlement gathering herbs, blossoms of wildflowers, roots, and twigs. In captivity to the Indians he has learned how to use these simple objects of nature for medical purposes. Chillingworth expresses great concern over Dimmesdale's health. No longer does Dimmesdale put his hand over his heart as an occasional, "casual gesture"; this gesture now has become a "constant habit." Finally, the young minister agrees to consult with Chillingworth. The two men take long walks while Dimmesdale unburdens his mind to the physician, but at no time does he mention what might be troubling his heart. Chillingworth attempts to probe. A great intimacy grows up between the two men, but still their companionship is based on their discussions of philosophy, of religion, of those things they both see in the world about them. Finally, Chillingworth moves into the house occupied by Dimmesdale. The young minister's rooms are hung with tapestry. The physician-scientist's rooms are arranged as a study and laboratory. Some people are delighted that Dimmesdale has the constant companionship of the physician, but many people, by instinct, begin to distrust Roger Chillingworth. They remember that when he came to town, his face was calm. Now there is "something ugly and evil" in his expression. Some people even go so far as to suggest that Roger Chillingworth might be haunting the young minister as a representative of the devil.

COMMENT
What a strong personality Roger Chillingworth is! He

comes to Boston to claim his bride and to live happily forever after with her. He discovers her shame (adultery), and then he promptly and privately disowns her. He substitutes a new goal—to discover the identity of his wife's lover. How carefully he plans his campaign. He fits beautifully into the scheme of things in Boston, for there is great need for a doctor. He soon becomes the close friend of Reverend Arthur Dimmesdale, who seems in need of medical attention. However, even after Chillingworth moves into the same house with Dimmesdale, the young minister does not completely unburden his heart to his companion and friend. Dimmesdale begins the habit of placing his hand over his heart, as if he feels a pain there. (See the beginning of Chapter XXIV, where the discussion centers around the possibility that Dimmesdale has a self-inflicted wound over his heart.) The tapestry hangings in Dimmesdale's apartment are symbolic, for the characters shown in the tapestry parallel those in our story: David resembles Dimmesdale, Bathsheba resembles Hester, and Nathan the Prophet is similar to Chillingworth.

THE SCARLET LETTER
CHAPTERS X–XIV

CHAPTER X: "THE LEECH AND HIS PATIENT"

This chapter is a continuation of the preceding chapter, with the exception that both the minister and his physician engage in dialogue, whereas in the preceding chapter there was almost no dialogue. Chillingworth digs into Dimmesdale's heart "like a miner searching for gold." During their conversations he learns of many things concerning Dimmesdale's thoughts: his hopes for mankind; his love of souls; his pureness of sentiment; and his natural holiness. And yet with all this, Chillingworth feels intuitively that Dimmesdale is hiding something. It is strange that the minister does not suspect his doctor of being more curious than he should be.

One day, in Chillingworth's laboratory, the two men fall into a casual conversation about some dark, flabby herbs that Dimmesdale has recently gathered. Very pointedly the physician says that the herbs were found growing on a grave; in fact, they probably have grown "out of" the heart of a dead man, representing "some hideous secret that was buried with him, and which he had done better to confess during his lifetime." (The physician is casting out a strong hint, encouraging the minister to talk about himself.) Dimmesdale replies that possibly the dead man desired "to confess," but he could not do so. He continues by saying that at the Judgment Day the man will confess "with a joy unutterable." Chillingworth says that the guilty one might achieve "solace," or relief, now. Why should he wait? Dimmesdale agrees in theory with the "leech," as he remembers watching "relief" on the faces of many people who had confessed their sins to him before their deaths. He goes on to explain (in one of the key passages of the book) that some sinners "shrink from displaying themselves black and filthy in the view of men." He explains that confession of past evil might make it impossible for them to continue serving "their fellow-creatures." Thus, these unhappy sinners daily walk around "looking pure as new-fallen snow; while their hearts are all speckled and spotted" with sin. Chillingworth vigorously answers that a "false show" cannot be better "than God's own truth." Dimmesdale says that this is possibly very true, and then he changes the subject to his own state of health.

At this time the two men hear the "clear, wild laughter" of a young child's voice, coming from the burial ground next door. They see Pearl dancing from one grave to another. In answer to her mother's demand that she behave, Pearl takes some prickly burrs from a burdock and then arranges them "along the lines of the scarlet letter" on her mother's bosom. Chillingworth remarks that there is "no law . . . mixed up with that child's composition." Dimmesdale thoughtfully answers that the child enjoys "the freedom of a broken law." Over-hearing the conversation, Pearl throws one of the prickly burrs at Dimmesdale. He shrinks back. Pearl claps her hands in childish ecstasy. (This is a dramatic moment, for the four main characters of the book look at one another in silence. Seldom are all four characters on the scene at the same time.) Pearl breaks the spell by urging her mother to come away, or else "yonder old Black Man" might catch her. The child adds that the Black Man has "got hold of the minister already." (Note how the intuition of the small child allows her to sense the true situation existing between the two men.) The mother and child leave, as Chillingworth questions whether Hester Prynne is "less miserable" because she wears the scarlet letter for all to see. Speaking of himself, Chillingworth says that to show one's pain is better "than to cover it all up in his heart."

At this point Chillingworth bluntly asks Dimmesdale if the sick minister has told his physician everything that might concern his case. Dimmesdale says all has been told. Chillingworth declares that sometimes a "bodily disease" may be only a "symptom" of a spiritual ailment. He then asks if the minister cares to "lay open to him the wound or trouble" in his soul.

Dramatically Dimmesdale cries out, "No!—not to thee!—not to an earthly physician!" He says he will assign himself to his God. Then he leaves, angry. Chillingworth watches his friend leave, remarking to himself that Dimmesdale is capable of sudden and unusual "passion." He then speculates that very likely the minister has before this time "done a wild thing . . . in the hot passion of his heart."

Eventually, the two men become friends again. One day, Chillingworth walks quietly into his friend's apartment. He finds Dimmesdale fast asleep. Advancing to his patient, the doctor removes the "vestment" that covers the top of the sleeping man's chest. Chillingworth stares and stares—then he turns away. The doctor's face reflects "wonder, joy, and horror . . . rapture." He throws his arms into the air; he stamps his feet on the floor. In his ecstasy, he resembles Satan.

COMMENT

Note that Chillingworth begins his search for Hester's lover with the feeling that he only wants to reveal the "truth." Before he knows it, he is overcome by a "terrible fascination," which forces him to probe and dig into the heart of his suspected victim (Dimmesdale). Finally, he is a man seeking a devilish revenge. He wishes the minister to suffer pangs of conscience, to be aware of his own (Dimmesdale's) hypocrisy. This chapter contains much dialogue between the two men as they fence with each other—Chillingworth constantly attempting to corner Dimmesdale, and Dimmesdale always offering vague and general explanations for the leech's probing, personal questions. Very often in the dialogue, when the minister is speaking of the "relief" that comes after the "outpouring" of confession, he shows how very much he would like to have that same "relief" (that "joy unutterable") through confession of his sins. In a key speech, Dimmesdale does explain why a sinner (of spotless reputation) might not confess: such a person would lose his "pure" reputation and would no longer be able to serve others. He would be held in general contempt. (One wonders how much of Dimmesdale's point of view is due to his wish for service and how much is determined by his unwillingness to be disgraced.)

How very cleverly Hawthorne breaks into the dialogue with the brief scene showing Pearl dancing in the graveyard. The presence of Pearl (who is indirectly being discussed) adds to, or heightens, the dramatic effect of the conversation. At the end of the chapter, Chillingworth looks at Dimmesdale's chest and sees something there that brings him "ecstasy." At last, he has some proof that the unhappy clergyman should be the victim of his revenge.

CHAPTER XI: "THE INTERIOR OF A HEART"

Chillingworth, now convinced that Dimmesdale is the guilty party, decides to have a terrible revenge on the minister. His plan is to "make himself the one trusted friend" of Dimmesdale, the one who will receive in confidence the minister's fears, remorse, agony, and repentance. The physician gloats over the idea that he, "the Unforgiving," will listen to the cries of "the Pitiless." Yet one thing does upset this plan a bit, and that is Dimmesdale's "shy and sensitive reserve." But to overcome this, the watchful doctor chooses his time carefully to suggest subtly some idea that will fill the minister with fear. For the most part Dimmesdale does not realize that he is being manipulated, much as a mouse is played with by a cat. Once in a while his instinct tells him everything is not right, and for a moment he looks with "horror" at the deformed Chillingworth. However, on the surface seeing nothing wrong with the old man, Dimmesdale blames himself for not truly appreciating his physician friend. The sense of hypocrisy in Dimmesdale has had an unusual effect on his preaching. His daily agony has made him sensitive to the needs, trials, and distress of others. He becomes increasingly famed among the Boston clergy. Some of his fellow ministers are greater scholars than he, some have sturdier minds, some have a greater spiritual presence, but Dimmesdale surpasses them all in one way: he possesses the "Tongue of Flame," for he is able to interpret humble, commonplace, familiar things of the ordinary world as having spiritual significance. Dimmesdale's congregation believe him to be "a miracle of holiness." The ground on which he walks they believe to be "sanctified."

Young maidens of his church find him irresistible. The aged members of the congregation greatly admire him. In the face of all this admiration Dimmesdale longs "to speak out, from his own pulpit, at the full height of his voice," telling the people the truth about himself: "I . . . am utterly a pollution and a lie!" Several times Dimmesdale draws a long breath in his pulpit, ready to tell his hearers that he is "altogether vile." He does tell them that he is vile, but he never gets to the place in the sermon when he explains why he is unworthy. (This is a form of hypocrisy, for he realizes he has no true intention of telling the complete truth.) His conscience does bother him, however, and he spends long nights in agony considering his sin. Sometimes he takes from a secret closet a "bloody scourge" (a whip with sharp particles attached to it). As he whips himself, he laughs bitterly. He fasts, going without food for long periods of time. He sits alone in total darkness through long nights. He varies this last activity by sometimes "viewing his own face in a looking-glass" with the aid of a powerful light. This "constant introspection" (looking inwardly at himself) tortures him but does not purify him. At times, his brain becomes weary, and "visions" flit across the surface of the looking glass; sometimes he sees demons who beckon to him; at other times he sees angels who look sorrowfully at him; and then he views "dead friends of his youth," his father and his mother; finally, he sees Hester Prynne leading Pearl by the hand. Everything has a bitterness about it to Dimmesdale. He realizes that he is an "untrue man," for as far as he is concerned "the whole universe is false." One night when he is particularly unhappy, Dimmesdale gets up from his chair and prepares himself to leave the house.

COMMENT

This is one of the key chapters of the book. We see Arthur Dimmesdale egged on by Chillingworth. We are given the generalization that the guilty minister suffers many tortures as the result of his hypocrisy. Then we are given the specific details concerning his torment. He uses the "scourge" (whip) to satisfy himself that not only Hester, but he, too, is suffering because of his sin with Hester. This active, physical torture is followed by another type of agony, this time a slower sort of punishment—the fast. He goes without eating until his body trembles with weakness. Keeping midnight "vigils" (watches), he sometimes suffers in darkness. At other times, he studies his face in a mirror with the help of a powerful light. This act of carefully looking at himself in a mirror is parallel to what happens daily in his life: his conscience looks at him and declares him a sinful hypocrite. Hester is able to externalize (put on the outside) her sin (adultery) by openly wearing the scarlet letter. But he feels he must always hide his guilt, and so he suffers from introspection (looking at and analyzing his own emotions).

CHAPTER XII: "THE MINISTER'S VIGIL"

Dimmesdale mounts the scaffold seven years after Hester had stood on it for penance. It is Saturday, on a dark night in early May. It is about midnight. He is drawn to Hester's scaffold of penance by "remorse." The fact that it is at night is representative of his "cowardice." Suddenly he shrieks aloud. He thinks he will awaken the whole town, but he does not do so. Only two people respond to his cry—the old magistrate, Governor Bellingham, and his sour-faced sister, Mistress Hibbins. The two people awakened by his cry finally go back to bed. Reverend Wilson is seen walking along carrying a dim lantern. This worthy minister has just come from the "death-chamber" of Governor Winthrop. Dimmesdale imagines that he speaks to the Reverend John Wilson, but he does not, for his mind is now playing tricks on him. He begins to think that he might not be able to leave the scaffold (because his limbs are beginning to grow stiff with the cold), and he imagines many early risers finding him crouched on the platform in the morning. He pictures elderly leaders of the community, as well as Governor Bellingham and Mistress Hibbins, all staring at him on the platform. He imagines "Father Wilson," the elders and deacons of his church, and Boston's purest young maidens turning their amazed faces up toward him. Almost hysterically, he laughs. His laugh is answered by a "light, airy, childish laugh," belonging to Pearl.

Hester and Pearl are just returning from Governor Winthrop's deathbed where Hester has "taken his measure for a robe." At Dimmesdale's invitation the two newcomers climb the steps of the platform. Quietly the minister takes one of Pearl's hands; Hester takes the child's other hand. It is a still moment. Pearl inquires if the minister will join them tomorrow noon in the same place. The minister says he cannot, but that he will join hands with the two at "the great judgment." (Dimmesdale soothes his own conscience by such a plan; that is, to confess his sins when all sins of the world are to be accounted for, according to his Puritan doctrine.) All at once, a meteor flashes through the sky, lighting all about them. To the guilty Dimmesdale the meteor has the "appearance of an immense letter,—the letter A." (Dimmesdale has adultery on his mind and his "guilty imagination" makes him connect this sin with everything around him.) Not only does this sudden flash of light reveal Pearl holding by each hand one of her parents, but it also reveals (especially to Pearl) the figure of Roger Chillingworth standing near the scaffold scowling at them like an "arch-fiend."

Instinctively, Dimmesdale gasps, "Who is that man, Hester?" A moment later, he says, "I have a nameless horror of the man."

He appeals to Hester to help him. Pearl mumbles into the minister's ear some childish "gibberish," in an attempt to identify Chillingworth. When Dimmesdale asks if she mocks him, she replies that he did not promise to take her mother's hand and her own hand in the noonday sun in front of other people. At this point, Chillingworth explains that he has spent the "better part of the night" at the bedside of the dying Governor Winthrop. He then demands that Dimmesdale accompany him home. The two leave together.

On the next day, the Sabbath, Dimmesdale preaches his finest sermon to date. As he leaves his pulpit, the church sexton holds up to him his own black glove as he explains that it had been found on the scaffold where it was probably dropped by Satan. The sexton also provides an interpretation of the meteor. He believes the letter *A* stood for "Angel," because Governor Winthrop became an angel when he died.

COMMENT

Driven by remorse and conscience, Dimmesdale goes to the marketplace and climbs the steps of the scaffold. He feels that he must stand in the very place where Hester humiliated herself by being stared at and abused by the townspeople. Being here will perhaps help relieve his pain and salve his conscience. Since he has dressed himself as he dresses when he preaches, he might possibly have in the back of his mind that he will be discovered by indignant members of his congregation who will publicly accuse him of sin and end his torture. His cry into the night only awakens Governor Bellingham and his sister, Mistress Hibbins. This attempt to draw attention to himself as a sinner is as ineffective as his previous unsuccessful efforts when he tried to confess in the pulpit. In this key scene, which is important in the development of the plot and the characters, the four main characters are brought face to face in a dramatic situation. Hester, Pearl, and Dimmesdale, when they hold hands on the scaffold, form a dramatic tableau (a picture that has some special significance, appearing as if it were posed, as people pose to have a picture taken). In this case the family relationship is emphasized, as Pearl stands between her parents, holding a hand of each. Dimmesdale refuses Pearl's request that on the following day in public he repeat this tableau (the symbolic holding of hands). Chillingworth, the fourth important character, stands watching them near the scaffold. By pointing her finger at the villain (Chillingworth), Pearl makes him an important part of the scene. How dramatic the moment is when the meteor (perhaps a shooting star) makes the night as bright as day to reveal the four characters together! History tells us that Governor Winthrop died in 1649. We know Pearl is seven years old at this time. Thus, we can date the beginning of the story as 1642.

CHAPTER XIII: "ANOTHER VIEW OF HESTER"

Hester realizes that there is a force damaging Dimmesdale's sense of peace other than his conscience alone. She realizes that Chillingworth is that evil force. Over a period of seven years her scarlet letter had become a "familiar object to the townspeople." To her credit she had never fought the public; she has always submitted "to its worst usage." For seven years her life has been "blameless." She has given generously to the poor and has nursed the sick. Many people begin to consider her a "Sister of Mercy." The letter *A* begins to become the symbol of her "helpfulness," meaning to some people not adultery but "able." Hester never demands public approval. Where there is darkness, sickness and poverty, there she is. Hers is not an existence filled with sunshine; hers is a dark world. The magistrates (judges) gradually begin to recognize her helpfulness.

One sacrifice has been made by Hester through the wearing of the scarlet symbol—she has lost much of her femininity.

Her somber looks, her hair hidden under a cap, and her reserved manner cause her to seem very stern. Of course, the fact that she once had allowed herself to be tender and has suffered considerably because of that influences her behavior now. She must not seem a loose woman in any way. If she were alone, she might have difficulty in keeping her solitary, stern position. But Pearl has caused her to carefully regulate her behavior. (If Hester were to live at a later period in history, she would probably be known as a feminist, a champion of women's rights.) Although Hester presents a submissive appearance, to the great satisfaction of her fellow Puritans, inwardly she lives in darkness and receives no comfort. Evidently, the scarlet letter represents a certain form of public penance, but it has not truly purified.

Her knowledge of sorrow helps her understand the great sadness in Dimmesdale's heart. She decides to help him. She knows that Chillingworth, Dimmesdale's "secret enemy," has falsely been pretending to be a "friend and helper" to the unhappy minister. Until this time she has had her lips sealed regarding her association with Chillingworth, for the vengeful old man had demanded this of her when he visited her seven long years ago in the prison. Hester makes up her mind to meet Chillingworth and talk the matter over with him. One afternoon, she finds him as he is walking, gathering roots and herbs for medical supplies.

COMMENT

Over a period of seven years since the birth of Pearl, Hester's reputation in the community has improved greatly. Her good deeds have caused many of the Puritans to change their original interpretation of the scarlet letter. Now some speak of Hester's willingness to help others and her strength. (The Puritans believed in faith in religion, emphasizing belief in the Bible more than good works. Hester gets their admiration for her good works.) Since Hester is not allowed to feel emotional about problems of the day, she spends her time thinking. She thinks much about the suffering of Dimmesdale. She finally decides that she must try to help him.

CHAPTER XIV: "HESTER AND THE PHYSICIAN"

First, Hester tells Pearl to run to the edge of the shore and play. The child stops at a pool of water left by the "retiring tide," and peeps in at the water mirror. Pearl finds herself looking at an elfish playmate, mirrored back at her from the water. She beckons to the playmate to join her, but the elfish maiden in the water beckons back to Pearl.

Chillingworth tells Hester that one of the magistrates has been discussing the question of her removing the scarlet letter from her breast. Hester tells the old man that it is not the place of the magistrates "to take off this badge." She also says that if she were worthy of having it removed, "it would fall away of its own nature." Hester is shocked to see how much Chillingworth has changed in several years. Once he was quiet and studious; now his expression is "almost fierce," and he has a false smile. At times, a red light seems to gleam out of his eyes. He has enjoyed his seven years of torturing Dimmesdale.

Hester tells him that she feels a duty toward Dimmesdale to tell him of Chillingworth's identity, that he is her husband. She further tells the old physician that he has caused Dimmesdale "to die daily a living death." She adds that she "acted a false part" when she agreed to hide Chillingworth's identity. The old man says, "What choice had you?" Chillingworth tells of the great effort he has put forth in caring for the ill minister's health. Then he gloats as he says that he has "grown to exist only by this perpetual poison of the direst revenge!"

Suddenly the old man realizes the depths of evil to which he has sunk—it is as if he were truly seeing himself in a mirror for the first time. Hester asks if Dimmesdale has not been punished enough. The physician cries out, "No!" Gloomily he tells of his own happy days in the past when he worked "faithfully for the advancement of human welfare." He says that he is a "fiend." Hester remarks that she did this to him, and she wonders why he has not revenged himself on her. He says to her, "I have left thee to the scarlet letter." Hester then firmly tells Chillingworth that she intends to reveal his identity to the suffering Dimmesdale. She asks the physician if he would not like "to pardon" the man who has wronged him—Dimmesdale. He answers that it is not in his power to do this, explaining that it is his fate to hate and torture Dimmesdale.

COMMENT

Notice in the first paragraph another one of Hawthorne's mirrors—this time a water mirror. Pearl looks at a pool of water and sees her own "elf smile" peep back at her. At this point in the story, we see Chillingworth completely changed from the kindly scholar pictured in Chapter II. An evil-faced man with a false smile, he welcomes the opportunity to discuss Dimmesdale with Hester. He claims to have preserved Dimmesdale's life by his medical attentions—all for the purpose of continuing to have a victim for his (Chillingworth's) revenge. (Compare this with one of his comments in Chapter IV, when he tells Hester that he wishes her to live so that she might still be shamed by wearing the scarlet letter.) This chapter contains one of the turning points of the book, for Hester makes the decision that she must tell Dimmesdale who his enemy is. Then she informs the "enemy" (Chillingworth) of what she plans to do.

THE SCARLET LETTER
CHAPTERS XV–XX

CHAPTER XV: "HESTER AND PEARL"

Hester wonders if a circle of shadow moves along around Chillingworth as he gathers his herbs. She says bitterly, "I hate the man!" She tries to stop herself from thinking further about her dislike of Chillingworth. She remembers her life with him nine years ago in Europe. Yet every memory that at one time might have been happy now seems to be ugly and sad. She wonders how she could have been persuaded to marry him. Then she declares aloud, "He betrayed me! He has done me worse wrong than I did him!" She is thinking of the fact that she, an innocent young woman, married an elderly scholar with whom she had very little in common. Hester feels no sorrow for Chillingworth's misery.

All this time, Pearl is keeping herself busy at the edge of the water. She flirts with herself in the water mirror. She makes boats out of birch bark. She captures tiny sea creatures stranded on the shore. She throws up white foam into the air, chasing after it as the breeze blows it here and there. Finally, she picks up tiny pebbles and throws them at beach birds. She believes she has broken the wing of one of the creatures. Then she settles down to gather seaweed to make herself look like a mermaid. Using eel grass she forms a bright green *A*. Hester comes on the scene and sees her child with a green *A* on her breast. She asks the child if she has any idea why her mother is wearing the scarlet letter. Pearl replies, "It is for the same reason that the minister keeps his hand over his heart!" She adds that the old man Hester has been talking with (Chillingworth) will know why the minister does this. For a moment Hester thinks she may be able to tell Pearl why she does wear the letter on her bosom, but she finally decides she cannot inform the child. She says that she knows little of the minister's heart and that she wears the scarlet letter "for the sake of its gold thread." This is the first time in seven years that Hester has suggested that the scarlet letter does not represent adultery. As a part of her penance, she had accepted the meaning given to the letter by the authorities.

During the evening, and just before Pearl goes to bed, Pearl questions her mother about the meaning of the scarlet letter. In the morning she repeats the question "Why does the minister keep his hand over his heart?"

COMMENT

Notice that now Hester has very unpleasant memories of her past life with Chillingworth. She blames him for marrying her. Pearl, the elflike child, all this time has been very much enjoying the sight of her own reflection in the pool of water. Then she takes eel grass and forms it into a green letter *A* on her childish breast. Much of the conversation in this chapter between the mother and child takes place because of this green letter. Pearl, for some unknown reason, connects her mother's scarlet letter with the minister's putting his hand over his heart. Hester wonders, at this point, if she might make a confidante of Pearl. Perhaps she can tell her of some part of her sorrow. Then she realizes that she cannot do this. When she says to the child that she wears the symbol "for the sake of its gold thread," it is the first time she has ever denied the meaning of her scarlet letter. In the manner of a child, Pearl continues to question her mother about the meaning of the letter and, also, of the minister's keeping his hand over his heart. Hester brushes aside the questions.

CHAPTER XVI: "A FOREST WALK"

For a few days after her talk with Chillingworth, Hester tries to meet Dimmesdale accidentally on one of his solitary walks. Never do their paths seem to cross. Finally she hears that he has gone to visit the Apostle Eliot, who is in the forest among the Indians whom he has converted to Christianity. Hester takes this opportunity to meet him.

She and Pearl walk to the forest. The sunlight dances to and fro among the trees, once in a while shining on little Pearl— but never shining on Hester. Pearl tells her mother that the sunlight "will not flee" from her because she wears nothing on her bosom yet. Hester tells her that she hopes the child will never wear such an ornament on her breast. Innocently, Pearl asks if the letter will not "come of its own accord" when she is a grown woman. Her mother answers her by sending her to play in the sunshine. Hester approaches the child, and as she nears the circle of light the sunshine vanishes.

Pearl then asks her mother to tell her a story about the Black Man. She inquires whether her mother has ever met the famous Black Man. Hester asks how the child knows about the Black Man. It seems that when Hester was watching near a sickbed in a neighboring house the previous evening, an old woman talked about the Black Man and mentioned that many people had "written in his book." Mistress Hibbins was one of the persons said to have written in the Black Man's evil volume. The old woman the previous night also said (reports the child) that the scarlet letter is the Black Man's mark on Hester. The child also reports that Hester is said to meet the evil one in the forest at night. Hester denies having left the child alone and tells her that she has met the Black Man once in her lifetime. She quietly says, "This scarlet letter is his mark!"

All this time the mother and child have been following the bank of a stream. Pearl speaks to the stream, asking why its voice is so very sad. The mother tells Pearl she hears a footstep on the path. She wishes Pearl to play in that place while she goes to speak with the new arrival. Pearl again asks her mother about the Black Man and suggests that the evil one has placed a mark on the minister's chest. She asks why the Reverend Dimmesdale does not wear "his mark" on the outside (on his clothing), as Hester does. Pearl wanders along listening to the babbling of the stream. Hester, remaining in the shadows cast by the trees, watches Dimmesdale come toward her along the forest path. She notes his feeble appearance. He looks aimless, as if he were truly ready to die and be finished with life. He keeps his hand over his heart.

COMMENT

This brief chapter helps set the stage for Hester's interview with Dimmesdale (which is the topic of the following two chapters). Hester has chosen the forest as a place where she might best meet the minister, for they will be less disturbed in the freedom of the forest than they might be in the town. Chillingworth's "interference" must be avoided. The minister has been on a visit to the Apostle Eliot, who has spent much of his life preaching to the Indians and making Christian converts. (John Eliot, Apostle to the Indians, is a historical personage.) The use of the sun as a symbol is notable here: Pearl plays in the sunshine, for she has not sinned; the sunlight disappears when Hester enters the scene, for she has sinned. The little brook is not only a part of the forest setting; it is used as a parallel to Pearl and her life. For instance, the brook comes from a "mysterious" wellspring and travels through "scenes" shadowed by the gloomy forest. As for Pearl, her origin is partly mysterious (insofar as the identity of her father is concerned), and her life with her mother has gloomy moments (when the Puritan children and their parents are not pleasant toward them). At the end of the chapter when Hester sees Dimmesdale approach through the forest, the minister looks as if he were ready to die. Hester has decided to come to his rescue at the right time.

CHAPTER XVII: "THE PASTOR AND HIS PARISHIONER"

When Hester first speaks to Dimmesdale in the forest he is very surprised, for he is not quite sure that a human being is talking to him. Hester's somber clothing and the heavy foliage cause her to be seen with difficulty. The two lovers address each other wonderingly, almost as if each doubted that the other lived. In one way, each seems to be a "ghost" to the other. As they look into each other's faces, they see mirrored some of their own sorrow. Arthur touches Hester's hand. This, at least, makes them feel they are living creatures in the same world.

They sit on a heap of moss and talk in general terms about the weather and each other's health. Gradually, they approach the topic on the mind of each; that is, the effect of their sin on their present happiness. He tells her that he has no peace— he has "nothing but despair." He explains that if he were a man without conscience, filled with "coarse and brutal in- stincts," he would have peace at the moment. He summarizes his position by pitifully saying, "Hester, I am most miserable!" Hester points out to him that the people "reverence" him and that he does much good among the members of his congre- gation. He answers that he looks inward at himself and sees the "black reality" the people are admiring. He says there is great "contrast" between what he seems and what he is. Hester tells him that his "good works" have helped prove his repen- tance, that he should have peace because of them. He says this is not so. He tells Hester that she wears the scarlet letter "openly" upon her bosom. His letter "burns in secret." He admits that he is greatly relieved to be able to look into the eyes of a person (Hester) who sees him for what he is. He wishes he had one friend (or one enemy) to whom he could daily reveal himself as a sinner. Hester tells him she could be the friend; then she tells him that he has an enemy who lives under the same roof as he. The minister clutches at his heart and is speechless for a while.

Now Hester realizes how much harm she is responsible for, because she has not told him of the constant presence of his enemy. She suddenly realizes that Chillingworth's prodding could very easily push the suffering minister toward insanity. Hester realizes that she still loves Arthur. The truth dawns on her. The loss of Dimmesdale's reputation—even death itself—would be better than the living torment that the unhappy minister is in. She tells him that she has been truthful about all things, except for revealing Chillingworth's identity to him. Then she says: "That old man—the physician! . . . he was my husband!" Dimmesdale throws Hester a black, fierce frown. Then he sinks to the ground and buries his face in his hands. He says that he should have known this, for he has found the sight of Chillingworth distasteful. He says, "Woman . . . I cannot forgive thee!" Hester cries, "Thou shalt forgive me!" Then tenderly she throws her arms about him and caresses him. Finally, he says that he forgives her.

Dimmesdale then says that there is one sin worse than his sin (of hypocrisy). That sin is the vengefulness of Chillingworth. Then the unhappy minister explains why Chillingworth is a very great sinner. It is because "he has violated, in cold blood, the sanctity of a human heart." He refers to the old physician's probing into his own heart. The two sit side by side, hand in hand, gazing at each other. All at once a thought crosses his mind. He realizes that Chillingworth knows Hester's "purpose to reveal" his real identity. (Chillingworth will know that Dimmesdale distrusts him.) The minister wonders if the fiendish old man will keep this a secret. Hester says that she thinks he will but that he will find other means of annoying Dimmesdale.

Dimmesdale is completely frustrated and just about decides to give up hope completely. He asks Hester to help him. Hester tells him that he does not need to stay in Boston. He can go into the wilderness, or he can go back to England or perhaps some other part of Europe. Dimmesdale says that he is "powerless to go." Hester says he must "begin all anew!" She even suggests that he might change his name and build a proud reputation under some other name. He answers that he has "not the strength of courage left" to go into the "wide, strange, difficult world, alone." She whispers, "Thou shalt not go alone!"

COMMENT

This is the first time that Hester Prynne and Arthur Dimmesdale have been together since the midnight watch on the scaffold. At that time they had been observed by Pearl and Chillingworth. Now they are alone, for Pearl is playing at some distance in the forest. It is a relief for Dimmesdale to admit to Hester that he is a hypocrite. She comforts him. But then she startles him by informing him that his friend Chillingworth is his enemy. He is angry with her for not telling him sooner. Finally, he forgives her. He begins to feel sad, for he has the idea that there is no hope for him in the future. Hester again comforts him, explaining that he need not flee alone. The whole chapter is a series of emotional shifts for Dimmesdale. He is sad; he is angered; he is depressed. In each case, he is given comfort by Hester. They both agree Chillingworth's sin of vengeance is worse than any of their sins.

CHAPTER XVIII: "A FLOOD OF SUNSHINE"

Hester for seven long years has been looking at the life around her from the point of view of a spectator. Dimmesdale, as a leading clergyman of Boston, looks at the same life that Hester views, but he is forced by the prejudices of the church to evaluate situations according to standard patterns of behavior. Hester, in a way, has freed herself by being solitary. On the other hand, Dimmesdale has become a prisoner of society. At first, Dimmesdale feels he should not go away from Boston, but finally he changes his mind and decides that he might enjoy a "better life" with Hester somewhere else. To his own surprise he feels a sudden joy. He wonders why this decision has not been arrived at sooner. Hester tells him not to look back. Then she undoes the clasp fastening the scarlet letter to her bosom and throws the symbol of shame on top of a pile of withered leaves. The letter almost falls into a small stream. Just as Dimmesdale immediately found happiness when he made the decision to go away with Hester, so does Hester find great relief by removing from her bosom the symbol of adultery. Impulsively, she takes off her cap and lets her long, dark hair fall around her shoulders. She smiles tenderly. Her beauty reappears. Then the sunshine starts to fill the forest around the two happy people. It would seem as if these two have the sympathy and approval of nature.

At this point, Hester is reminded of Pearl and tells Arthur that he must see her now with his new outlook. The minister is afraid that she will shrink away from him. Hester calls to Pearl, who is standing some distance away in the forest. The child starts slowly toward the mother. The little creatures of the forest do not seem to fear her. A partridge, a pigeon, a squirrel, a fox, and even a wolf all look at her and show no fear. Possibly these wild creatures recognize a "wildness in the human child" very much like their own. Pearl has gathered flowers. She walks very slowly toward her mother, for she sees Arthur Dimmesdale.

COMMENT
How Hester changes when she throws aside her scarlet letter! She frees her long hair from under her close cap. She smiles. She looks tender and womanly. The sun, which always before stayed away from her, now shines all about her. She is eager to have Pearl and Arthur meet and love each other. On the other hand, Pearl is not anxious to join her mother and the minister, for she is not altogether comfortable in the minister's presence. Also, her mother somehow seems changed. This chapter is a logical introduction to the following one because it ends as Hester and Arthur discuss Pearl. The next chapter pictures the three people together.

CHAPTER XIX: "THE CHILD AT THE BROOK-SIDE"
As Hester and Arthur watch Pearl while she is approaching, Hester mentions the fact that Pearl has inherited from Dimmesdale his "brow." Dimmesdale claims that he sees his

own features in her face—in fact, he has been afraid that "the world might see them." Hester and Dimmesdale are united in Pearl. She is a symbol of their love. The mother asks the father not to excite the child when he greets her. Hester feels that finally the child will love her father. Dimmesdale reminds Hester that he is not at his best with children. He does remember, however, Pearl's caressing his hand in Governor Bellingham's hall.

Pearl stands at the edge of a brook, silently gazing at the waiting pair, and her reflection in the water is a thing of beauty. In some ways, Hester feels herself separated from the child. The mother encourages the child to come to her, but the child does not respond to her. All at once, Dimmesdale places his hand over his heart. Then, Pearl stretches out her hand and points with her small forefinger at her mother's breast. (The water mirror exactly reproduces this scene—a young child, decorated by flowers, standing in a ray of sunlight and pointing her forefinger toward some distant object.) Hester again invites the child to come nearer. Pearl points. She frowns. She stamps her foot. She screams. All this time, Pearl's reflection is seen in the brook. (It is almost as if there were two children excited about something.) Then, Hester realizes what is the matter. She says, "Pearl misses something which she has always seen me wear."

Upset, the minister asks Hester to do something to quiet the child. He adds, "if thou lovest me." (Seldom has Dimmesdale allowed himself to be so affectionate in speech.) Hester tells the child to bring the scarlet letter to her. The child refuses. Then Hester takes up the letter and fastens it again to her bosom. She follows this by confining all of her hair beneath her cap. All at once her feminine warmness disappears. She is again the same somber Hester that she was earlier in the day. Then the child comes to her mother, kisses her, and even kisses the scarlet letter. The mother and child discuss the minister. Pearl wonders if Dimmesdale will return with them to the town, "hand in hand." Hester says he will not at this time, but eventually the three of them will have a "home and fireside" of their own. Pearl asks the inevitable question, "And will he always keep his hand over his heart?" Mother and daughter join the clergyman. He kisses Pearl on the brow. The child runs to the brook and scrubs the kiss from her forehead. Then she stays apart from them while they make arrangements for their future.

COMMENT

How very deep must be Dimmesdale's sense of guilt and hypocrisy if he thinks that people might recognize his features in little Pearl's face. The minister is almost afraid of Pearl (as he is of most children), but he does remember her moment of gentleness when she caressed his hand in Governor Bellingham's hall. Pearl lingers at the edge of a brook, where her reflection is mirrored in a small pool. The child looks almost like another being, as she hesitates in the sun at the edge of the pool. With childish directness she points toward what is causing her to be so slow in approaching her mother: it is the absence of the scarlet letter on Hester's breast. All of this scene is mirrored in the brook as Pearl has a tantrum, screaming, shrieking, pointing, and stamping. The mirroring of the scene makes it seem even twice as disturbing as it is. When Hester picks up the letter and pins it again on her dress, Pearl's anger disappears. But the happiness that has briefly been Hester's (with the removal of the scarlet letter) is also ended—Hester is once again a captive to shame and the scorn that society has prescribed for her. Notice the pattern of emotional rhythm in this story. Whenever one character is happy, it is more than likely that there is someone near (or involved with him or her) who is unhappy. Hawthorne often writes of contrasts in emotions.

CHAPTER XX: "THE MINISTER IN A MAZE"

At first, when Dimmesdale leaves Hester and Pearl in the forest, he cannot be sure that what has recently happened is really true. He thinks that perhaps he has been dreaming, but the sight of Hester and Pearl reminds him that he can take hope for the future. Arthur and Hester plan to go to the Old World. They plan to set sail on a vessel that has recently arrived from the Spanish Main. Their first destination will be Bristol, England. Through her nursing Hester has come to know the captain and some of the crew. Dimmesdale is happy that they will leave on the fourth day, for on the third day he is to preach the Election Sermon.

Excited, and filled with energy, Dimmesdale hurries back to town. Everything he sees looks different to him now, after his talk with Hester. This is because he himself has changed. Suddenly he has impulses to do strange or wicked things. First, he meets one of the oldest deacons of his church. He has to restrain himself from saying some vile things about the Communion Supper (the taking of the bread and the wine, one of the most sacred parts of the Puritan church services). Second, as he walks along he catches up with the eldest female member of his church. He finds that he must stop himself from breathing into her ear an "unanswerable argument against the immortality of the human soul." He mumbles something to her, and she throws him a look of "divine gratitude and ecstasy." Third, he meets the youngest female member of his congregation. He is tempted to whisper to her some evil thought that might eventually mislead her. He acts as if he does not recognize her, and he hurries onward. Fourth, Dimmesdale meets a group of children. He is tempted to stop and teach the little ones "wicked words." He restrains himself. Fifth, he meets a drunken sailor from the ship in the harbor. He wants to shake hands with the sailor and to throw a few oaths back and forth with him. He again succeeds in restraining himself. Sixth and finally, he meets Mistress Hibbins, who looks very grand, being richly decked out in a gown of velvet. The old woman speaks to him with great familiarity, suggesting that he has been in the forest to talk with the "Black Man." Dimmesdale tells her he has been to see his friend, the Apostle Eliot, who has been converting the Indians to Christianity. Mistress Hibbins does not believe him.

When Dimmesdale reaches his apartment, he looks around the walls. All at once he realizes that his customary surroundings look strange to him. Again he knows that he is a different man from the one who left this chamber earlier. A knock comes at the door and Roger Chillingworth enters. The physician asks about Dimmesdale's health. The minister then tells him that there will be no more need for Chillingworth's drugs. (He adds ironically to this, "good though they be, and administered by a friendly hand.") There is something in his tone that tells the old man that the young minister no longer considers him a "trusted friend" but that he now thinks of the physician as "his bitterest enemy." However, nothing is said on the surface of the conversation to indicate that the men are enemies. Chillingworth asks if he might use his medical powers to help make Dimmesdale "strong and vigorous" in preparation for the delivery of the Election Sermon on the next day. He adds that the people are afraid that with the arrival of another year they may find their minister gone. With double meaning again the minister says, "Yea, to another world." (Chillingworth does not realize at this time that Dimmesdale plans to go to "another world"—the Old World.) After Chillingworth leaves, Dimmesdale eats a hearty meal. Then he flings into the fire the Election Sermon he has already begun. With great "thought and emotion," he composes an inspired sermon. When dawn arrives, he is still writing.

COMMENT

Arthur Dimmesdale has suffered from so many unhappy dreams and visions that it seems quite natural when he doubts at first that he has just talked with Hester and

Pearl in the forest. He is very pleased that he will be able to deliver the Election Sermon on the day before they expect to leave for Europe. To be chosen to give this sermon is the highest honor any minister can have in seventeenth-century Boston. He convinces himself that he is glad to be able to fulfill his public duty by preaching on this very special occasion. Actually, he is very proud of himself and is overcome by false humility. (He resembles men who want to run for high political office but who tell people that they campaign because their friends insist on it.) Note how changed everything looks to Dimmesdale when he returns from the forest, all excited with his plans to leave Boston, his place of torture.

The six encounters he has on the way home are with people who are representative of different groups in the story. (This is somewhat like a review of many of the main characters near the end of the story.) The old deacon might stand for the ritual and ceremony of the church Dimmesdale has been connected with. The old woman is one of those who have considered him an earthly angel, as he has preached hope to her. The young maiden might resemble Hester Prynne who also was once young and innocent and a member of Dimmesdale's parish. The Puritan children have been seen several times before when they irritated Hester and Pearl. The drunken seaman is one of the last to be added to the tale, representing Arthur and Hester's plan for escape. Mistress Hibbins, with her knowing remarks about the Black Man, makes one think of little Pearl's often-repeated comment about Hester's scarlet letter and the Black Man of the forest. When Dimmesdale arrives home, he is ironic (saying one thing, and meaning another): he refers to Chillingworth's giving him drugs with a "friendly hand."

THE SCARLET LETTER
CHAPTERS XXI–XXIV

CHAPTER XXI: "THE NEW ENGLAND HOLIDAY"

Hester and Pearl arrive in the marketplace on the day of the holiday. Everywhere people are walking about. Even the settlers who live on the outskirts of the town have come to participate in the festivities. Hester is dressed quietly in coarse gray cloth. Her face is "like a mask." A keen observer might notice a small light in her face. Inside, she can whisper, "look your last on the scarlet letter and its wearer!" Hester thinks of herself as being on the high seas in a few hours, leaving Boston forever. Pearl is brightly dressed. She moves about "with a bird-like movement." Sometimes she bursts into wild shouts. She comments on all the workmen she sees in their best clothes. She wonders why Master Brackett, the old jailer, nods and smiles at her. Her mother tells her the old man remembers her as a child. Pearl notices the Indians and the sailors, and she wonders why they are there in the market-place. Her mother explains to her that all of these people are waiting to see the procession pass by. Pearl wonders if the minister will hold out his hands to her. Her mother tells her that he will not do this today. Almost to herself, the child comments that the minister is a "strange, sad man . . . with his hand always over his heart!"

Everybody seems to be filled with joy. The men are partici-pating in sports. Some are wrestling; some are in friendly matches with the quarter staff; some are opponents with swords. A party of Indians and some of the crew of the vessel stand watching the Puritans. The sailors are rough-looking men, dressed in colorful costumes. The captain of the vessel soon enters the marketplace in conversation with Roger Chillingworth, the physician. The captain is dressed in a suit covered with ribbons. He has gold lace on his hat, which is also encircled by a gold chain. The captain sees Hester Prynne, and, recognizing her, speaks to her. Hester is near no one at the time, for people generally stand away from her. The commander of the vessel explains to her that one more passenger is to take ship with them. He feels that he is very fortunate that a doctor will be traveling with them. Hester is startled. The captain continues his conversation, saying that Chillingworth will take ship with them. (Evidently Chillingworth has suggested that he is a close friend of Dimmesdale, and so the captain thinks everything will be all right if the physician accompanies his "friend.") Hester looks up, to see Roger Chillingworth smiling at her from a distant part of the marketplace. His smile fills her with fear.

COMMENT

This chapter contrasts in several ways with the few before it. For instance, the last chapters have been concerned with the feelings, thoughts, and actions of small groups of people—often only one or two at a time, such as Hester and Arthur. This chapter is filled with people—not only members of the Puritan community but also Indians from the forest and sailors from the distant seas. By introducing outside elements, such as the sailors, Hawthrone makes one more aware of the world outside Boston; therefore, Hester's *A* seems a bit less significant. Her trouble seems more like one happening among all the many happenings in a big world. Before this, most of the dialogue and action have centered around Hester's symbol of adultery. The seamen are described as being lawless in every way, and Hester's sin seems somewhat mild compared to acts the sailors might daily commit. This chapter provides a picture of Puritan times, and it shows how settlers in the New World enjoy some of the same physical activities as their relatives in the Old. For example, the people relax by participating in or watching sports, such as wrestling, duels with the quarter staff (long, heavy, iron-tipped pole), and exhibitions with the sword. After all the varied activity in the marketplace is pictured, the action simmers down again at the end of the chapter, when Hester is horrified to learn that Chillingworth knows of the planned escape by Arthur, Pearl, and herself. She is visibly distraught at the idea that he will sail with them.

CHAPTER XXII: "THE PROCESSION"

Before Hester can gather her wits about her after being shocked by the news that Chillingworth will accompany them on the ship, the procession is heard approaching. First comes the music, played by the drum and some light woodwind instruments. Pearl is thrilled at the sound. Next come the soldiers, most of whom are gentlemen dressed in soldiers' uniforms. (They resemble the modern National Guard.) They, too, are brilliantly dressed. Then are seen the magistrates (rulers) of the colony: Bradstreet, Endicott, Dudley, and Bellingham. The magistrates are followed by the minister who is to deliver the Election Sermon—Arthur Dimmesdale. He is a different Dimmesdale. His steps are not feeble; his body is not bent; his hand does not rest upon his heart. There is a spiritual look on his face. He looks deep in thought. Hester watches him closely. She remembers some of their past moments together. He does not seem to be the same man she has been encouraging with the thought of escaping Boston. Even little Pearl does not quite recognize him. She says that, if she had been sure who he was, she would have run to him and kissed him before all the people. Another observer of the procession is Mistress Hibbins, who is magnificently dressed with three ruffs around her neck, a gown of costly velvet, and a gold-headed cane. Mistress Hibbins whispers confidentially to Hester. She declares to Hester that Dimmesdale has been a part of the Black Man's group in the forest. Mistress Hibbins says that Hester wears her token of sin openly. She further declares that the minister hides his sin "with his hand always over his heart." With a shrill laugh the old gentlewoman leaves.

Hester does not enter the church. She stands near the scaffold, within listening distance of Dimmesdale who is delivering the sermon in the church. Although she cannot catch every word Dimmesdale speaks, Hester is aware of the general tone and spirit of what the minister is saying. She recognizes that a human heart is trying to reveal its secret, without specifically explaining all the details. While Hester listens, Pearl wanders about. The ship's master takes from his hat the gold chain that is twisted about it and throws it to the child. The captain sends a message to Hester by the child Pearl. It is that Chillingworth says he will bring Dimmesdale on board the ship with him and that Hester need only be concerned with Pearl and herself. Hester is surrounded by people from the country roundabout who have heard about the scarlet letter but who have never seen it. These spectators are joined by the sailors and the Indians and even some of the townspeople. The chapter ends as two of the most important people of the romance are both being observed—Hester by curious people who are staring at her scarlet letter, and Dimmesdale by an audience which has been greatly, emotionally affected by his passionate sermon.

COMMENT

The procession is one of Hawthorne's ways of bringing many of his characters together. The procession organized for the festivities before the Election Sermon is of this type. The music comes first, followed by soldiers (who maintain law and order). The group of governors and magistrates then makes its way along. In an honored position follows the representative of the church (in this case, Arthur Dimmesdale). Hester has helped give Arthur new courage. He has used this new courage to become more spiritual than ever before. Thus he does not see Hester (his inspiration and hope) as he marches in the procession. One sympathizes with Hester when she faintly resents his not noticing her. Yet Hester defends Dimmesdale when Mistress Hibbins criticizes him. The old "witch" has noted the same thing that has often been on little Pearl's mind; that is, the minister keeps putting his hand over his heart. Dimmesdale's sermon is not summarized for us, but the general import of it is known as Hester reacts to what she faintly hears. She is aware of the agony in the minister's voice. The pain in Dimmesdale's heart and soul is evident in his tones. The minister's anguish is matched by Hester when the ship captain sends a message to her through Pearl. Chillingworth plans to help Dimmesdale to board the ship. There seems to be little hope for Hester and Dimmesdale. They are to be followed by the fiend Chillingworth. There seems to be no escape.

CHAPTER XXIII: "THE REVELATION OF THE SCARLET LETTER"

As the chapter opens, Dimmesdale has just brought his sermon to a close. The audience is still. Then it pours out into the marketplace. In the open air the excited listeners begin to explain to each other how wonderful this Election Sermon has been. The subject of the sermon was the relationship between God and humanity, with special reference to people in New England. At the end of the sermon Dimmesdale prophesied a glorious future for the people of the Boston colony. The whole sermon had an undertone of sadness—almost as if their beloved minister were bidding good-bye to them before starting out on a journey. (This journey might well be death.) At this time, Arthur Dimmesdale stands at the most triumphant moment of his existence. This is the high point of his career as a minister. He bows his head on the cushions of the pulpit as the members of his congregation look at him idolatrously. Meanwhile, Hester Prynne is outside the meeting house and is circled by a curious group of spectators staring at the scarlet letter.

Now the music begins again, and the "military escort" falls into place. The procession has started. The magistrates and the governor, as well as the Boston ministers, are on their way to the town hall, where they will enjoy a "solemn banquet" to round out the ceremonies of the day. In the middle of the marketplace the parade is greeted by a loud roar of approval. The man who is being cheered most enthusiastically by the townspeople is Arthur Dimmesdale. All eyes turn toward him. The shouting dies into a murmur. He has changed within the last few minutes. His energy seems gone. His cheeks are pale. He walks as if he might fall at any moment. Reverend John Wilson offers to help him, but Dimmesdale refuses aid. Now he is opposite the scaffold. Dimmesdale pauses. The music being played for the procession urges him to continue "onward to the festival." But he stops. Governor Bellingham, upset, leaves his place in the procession in order to offer aid to Dimmesdale. The minister gives the magistrate a look that causes him to return to his original position among the other magistrates.

Arthur Dimmesdale turns toward the scaffold, stretches forth his arms, and says, "Hester, come hither! Come, my little Pearl!" He gives them a look full of tenderness. Pearl runs to him and clasps her arms about his knees. Hester draws near him but pauses before she reaches him. Suddenly, Roger Chillingworth pushes through the crowd and catches Dimmesdale by the arm, whispering, "Madman, hold! What is your purpose? Wave back that woman! Cast off this child! All shall be well!" Dimmesdale says, "Thou art too late!" He continues: "With God's help I shall escape thee now!" Then Dimmesdale calls on Hester to give him her "strength." He wants not only her spiritual strength but also her physical strength, so that she might help him climb to the platform of the scaffold. The crowd goes wild. They do not want to recognize the solution to this puzzle; they cannot allow themselves to believe that Dimmesdale has a close relationship to Hester and Pearl.

There are four people now standing on the scaffold—Hester, Arthur, Pearl and Roger Chillingworth. (Chillingworth finds he must be with the people he has been so closely associated with.) Dimmesdale tells Hester that he is about to die. He wishes to share her "shame." Then he passionately denounces himself to the spectators as he reveals that he is Pearl's father. He explains that he has his own "red stigma" very much like Hester's scarlet letter. With a violent motion he tears away the "ministerial band" at the top of his garment. The audience is shocked. (Evidently, Dimmesdale has been punishing himself by mutilating the flesh of his breast, sketching out a letter very much like Hester's *A*.) Dimmesdale sinks to the platform of the scaffold. Hester helps prevent him from falling. Chillingworth kneels beside him, saying, "Thou hast escaped me!" Dimmesdale asks God's forgiveness for the physician, adding that Chillingworth has also "deeply sinned." (This, of course, is a reference to Chillingworth's desire for revenge.)

Dimmesdale invites Pearl to kiss him. She does. Then the child cries, the tears flowing "upon her father's cheek." Hester wonders if she and Arthur will meet again in another life. Dimmesdale fears that they may not. He is grateful that God has been merciful to him by giving him the "burning torture to bear" upon his breast, by sending Chillingworth to torment him, and by encouraging him to confess on the scaffold. Then Arthur Dimmesdale dies.

COMMENT

This is the most dramatic chapter of the entire book. It is filled with high points. Dimmesdale finishes his sermon, and the people are almost stunned into silence with admiration at his brilliant, inspired thoughts. Then they outdo one another, loudly declaring that never before has man spoken so well. The procession of prominent people threads its way through the excited people. The townspeople cheer. Suddenly, in great contrast, is seen the changed figure of the minister. He no longer is strong and hearty. He almost staggers. How he has changed from what he was a few minutes ago, at the end of his triumphant sermon! He totters on his feet. Evidently, he is gathering his courage to do the thing that has represented horror and disgrace to him: he is about to confess. How dramatic is his beckoning to Hester and Pearl to join him! Even more dramatic is Roger Chillingworth's attempt to stop Dimmesdale from confessing. When the feeble minister calls on Hester to help him climb the steps of the scaffold, the crowd is very curious. Chillingworth instinctively follows them up the stairs to the platform of the scaffold, for he has been one of the "actors" in this "drama of guilt and sorrow." Dimmesdale refers to his "own red stigma," and then he pushes aside his clerical neckpiece and reveals it to the "horror-stricken multitude." (One never knows exactly what Dimmesdale's "stigma" is, but it might resemble the mark of a branding iron formed into the letter *A*. The minister refers to it as being the "type" of what has "seared" his own heart.) Arthur Dimmesdale has thus gained a strange sort of humility. He has faced up to the situation—that is, he has freely admitted his part in Hester's sin. He believes that he and Hester may never meet in a life after death. He is even grateful for the torture he has been through, for he feels that he has been saved (and forgiven) through his torment. Thus, he dies, believing he has paid the price for his sin through his suffering.

CHAPTER XXIV: "CONCLUSION"

Most of the spectators who watch and listen to Dimmesdale on the scaffold later agree that they had seen a scarlet letter on his breast. There is a variety of opinion as to how the letter came to be there. Some people believe Dimmesdale inflicted it on himself, as he daily endured torture with the knife. Others feel that the avenger, Chillingworth, had caused the letter to appear through the use of magic and drugs. Still others feel that remorse, "gnawing" from Dimmesdale's heart outward, finally appeared on the surface of his breast. A few people insist that Dimmesdale had no mark on his breast and that he spoke with Hester on the scaffold, to point out to the spectators that he humbly considered himself a sinner. The moral of the story is taken from Dimmesdale's experience. It is: "Be true! Show freely to the world, if not your worst, yet some trait whereby the worst may be inferred!"

After Dimmesdale's death Chillingworth loses his sense of direction. He has concentrated on revenge, and now that there can be no more revenge he has nothing to do. Within the year he dies, leaving Pearl a large amount of property both in America and in England. Pearl becomes "the richest heiress of her day in the New World." (Hawthorne suggests that now she might marry into any devout Puritan family, for her money makes her very attractive.)

Hester and Pearl soon leave the colony and are not heard of for a number of years. Finally, Hester reappears in Boston and takes up residence in the same little cottage she had occupied before. She even wears a scarlet letter on her breast. Pearl is not with her. People are not sure if she is alive, but gifts and letters come from Europe for Hester, indicating that someone of wealth has affection for her. Hester occupies a respected position in the Boston community. People bring their problems to her, particularly women unhappy in love. Hester soothes them. After many years Hester Prynne dies and is placed beside Arthur Dimmesdale in the burial ground. One tombstone serves both the lovers. How very suitable it is that the inscription (concerning a scarlet letter on a black background) should at last bring the two lovers together.

COMMENT

And so Hawthorne draws the threads of his story together, making sure that most of the reader's questions are answered. The spectators who witnessed Dimmesdale's confession on the scaffold do not all later agree as to what they have seen. Most of them agree that there was on Dimmesdale's breast a scarlet letter very much like Hester Prynne's. However, his was "imprinted in the flesh." Since people often see only what they want to see—and also believe only what they want to believe—there are different versions of this part of the tale. Some clearly saw; others definitely did not. Among those who saw, opinion is divided as to how the "red stigma" happened to appear on the minister's breast. Chillingworth has fed his whole soul on revenge. When Dimmesdale dies, there is no longer anyone to have revenge on, so he too dies within the year. He has much wealth (in property), which he wills to Pearl. Hester and Pearl disappear from Boston. In later years, Hester returns alone to her small cottage by the seashore where she again wears her scarlet letter and does many good deeds and gives good advice, especially to the women who suffer in love affairs or for lack of them. Letters and fine gifts from Europe indicate that someone there cares for Hester. On Hester's death, she is buried near Dimmesdale. The same tombstone, describing the scarlet ("gules") letter, serves both lovers.

CHARACTER ANALYSES

HESTER PRYNNE

Hester Prynne, Boston adulteress, is first seen (in Chapter II) as she comes from prison. The picture we have of her is almost as if it were in the words of one of the spectators who explains what he or she saw to someone who had to stay at home. The reporting spectator might say, "The young woman was tall, with a figure of perfect elegance, on a large scale. She had dark and abundant hair, so glossy that it threw off the sunshine with a gleam, and a face which, besides being beautiful from regularity of feature and richness of complexion, had the impressiveness belonging to a marked brow and deep black eyes. She was lady-like, too, after the manner of the feminine gentility . . . characterized by a certain state and dignity. . . . And never had Hester Prynne appeared more lady-like . . . than as she issued from the prison . . . her beauty shone out. . . ." The reporter continues about her clothing, saying that it "seemed to express the attitude of her spirit, the desperate recklessness of her mood, by its wild . . . peculiarity. But the point which drew all eyes . . . was that SCARLET LETTER, so fantastically embroidered . . . upon her bosom." The excited spectator finishes off this report by explaining that Hester Prynne seemed separated from everyone by the scarlet letter *A* on her bosom. She is separated from humankind. She appears dignified—almost pridefully so—but her spirit inside droops, and her heart is filled with agony. Finding no relief from the outside world, Hester has to seek help from the inside world, the world of her memories and her imagination. Thus, depending on her thoughts, she bears up under the public indignation at her adultery.

Throughout the story, Hester generally remains silent, accepting the abuse of Puritan parent and child alike. Only when public criticism threatens her two loved ones (Pearl and Dimmesdale) does she speak up to the Boston townspeople. She defends her ability to care for Pearl when she talks with

Governor Bellingham, one of the people planning to take the child from her. She speaks strongly to Chillingworth about his torturing Dimmesdale. She encourages Dimmesdale to flee the colony. She is well known for her submissiveness, for she never complains. She nurses and aids the poor; in return, they say bitter things to her, yet she accepts it all. She sews gorgeous garments for the Boston magistrates, and she wears very plain, coarse clothing. She submits to everything—on the outside. But inside, she is a different person. She feels that she is paying for her sin of adultery by accepting the criticism of the townspeople, as well as by wearing the scarlet letter on her breast. She submits every day; but inwardly, she is not truly sorry for her sin. She is isolated from her fellow human beings; she has little left to do but to think. She speculates about woman's place in the world. If she were not a sinner (having lost her good name through adultery), she would very likely be a leading fighter for women's rights (a feminist). She has few fears, for she has reached the bottom of the social ladder. Her one proud possession is her daughter, little Pearl, whom she dresses in brilliant colors representing her own spirit of inward resistance, although the child is the living symbol of her adultery. Since Hester is open to criticism from anyone in town, she finds she must appear unemotional. She wears her hair under a tight-fitting cap. Her natural womanly manner is completely covered. Only when she is with Pearl does she seem impulsive and warm. Otherwise, the public views her as a cold, bloodless statue.

Since Hester speaks relatively little, her few remarks are well chosen and well phrased. She speaks with calm detachment when she discusses Arthur Dimmesdale with Roger Chillingworth. After the physician has left her, she does break out with one bitter remark: "I hate the man!" When Hester feels the freedom of the forest, she relaxes to some extent. Prying eyes do not observe her there. As she removes her scarlet letter and lets down her long, dark hair from under her cap, she is immediately changed. Her feminine qualities, her youth, her beauty—all return to her. Then, at last, the sunshine pours down upon Hester. (The sun has always lingered around Pearl, but it always has disappeared with the approach of Hester and her scarlet letter.)

The story has a fitting ending, as one pictures Hester Prynne living to a ripe old age, always being helpful to those less fortunate than she, always consoling women whose hearts are filled with grief from unhappy love affairs—and always wearing her symbol (for "adulteress" turned to "able"): the scarlet letter.

ARTHUR DIMMESDALE

Hester Prynne's guilty partner in sin, Arthur Dimmesdale, does not make his appearance in the story until well into Chapter III. He is first seen through the eyes of the crowd viewing Hester Prynne's penance on the scaffold. He is pictured as if he were being described by one of the spectators for the benefit of a watcher of short stature, one who is not tall enough to see easily the impressive young minister. The running account goes something like this: The Reverend Arthur Dimmesdale is a "young clergyman . . . from one of the great English universities, bringing all of the learning of the age into our wild forest-land. . . . A person of very striking aspect, with a white, lofty . . . brow, large, brown, melancholy eyes, and a mouth . . . expressing . . . a vast power of self-restraint . . . . An air about this young minister,—an apprehensive, a startled, a half-frightened look,—as of a being . . . quite astray and at a loss in the pathway of human existence . . . only . . . at ease in some seclusion of his own." Arthur Dimmesdale often speaks in a voice that is "sweet, rich, deep, and broken." His message comes out through the sound of his voice, rather than through his words.

As the story progresses, Dimmesdale is very often found holding his hand over his heart. (It is very likely that he has a physical pain in the region of his heart, for in Chapter XXIII he reveals to the audience a red stigma—an unhealed wound in the form of a scarlet letter—over his heart.) Gradually he becomes more careworn, and his eyes have "a world of pain in their troubled and melancholy depths." In a conversation in Chillingworth's laboratory, Dimmesdale explains (in a veiled manner) why he cannot confess his part in Hester's sin. It is because he cannot reveal his sinfulness and then be allowed to keep on doing good works for men. People would be repulsed by him; they would have no more to do with him. This explanation is made, of course, as a reason why men—in general—do not confess their sins. Chillingworth suspects that the minister is the man he is looking for; but it is only later in the same chapter that he knows for sure, when he examines the wounded breast of the sleeping Dimmesdale. Arthur Dimmesdale begins to feel distrustful of Roger Chillingworth, although he can find no definite reason for this feeling.

Dimmesdale is very popular as a minister. One strong reason for this is his sympathy. His own sinful act has made him aware of the state of mind of the ordinary sinner. He communicates this sense of deep sympathy so that people begin to idolize him. Over and over again, he starts to confess his sin as he faces his Sunday congregation. In general terms, he speaks of his own great sin, but he always takes the coward's way out at the end of the sermon and finishes without confessing anything. Members of his parish return home from church declaring to each other how great their own sins must be if their sainted Reverend Dimmesdale considers himself a sinner. Dimmesdale, the hypocrite, eases his conscience by his midnight watches, alone in his chamber. Sometimes he scourges himself; sometimes he goes without food; and sometimes he closely examines his face in a well-lighted mirror. Since he knows himself to be a hypocrite, he is often quietly suspicious of the motives of people about him. Unable to endure his solitary guilt, in the middle of one May night he climbs the scaffold (where Hester stood in penance) and shrieks aloud, almost hoping he might be heard and discovered, and thus end his misery. He does make some progress toward his later confession, however, for he and Hester together hold little Pearl's hands, and he feels closer to the two than he has felt for some time.

Later in the forest, Arthur tells Hester of his great suffering—of his remorse and the pangs of conscience that torment him. When Hester informs him that Chillingworth is his enemy, he rouses himself enough to be angry at her for not telling him sooner. Using her womanly tenderness, she gains his forgiveness. Then the weak Dimmesdale begins to depend on the strong Hester for moral support. She persuades him that he and she and Pearl can flee the colony. He takes heart.

Here Dimmesdale begins to make some rapid changes in his point of view. On his way home from the forest, he is tempted to speak shocking words to Puritan men, women, and children as well as to the sailors of the vessel he plans to sail on. His experience with Hester has started to free him. He is actually exhilarated. After eating a hearty meal, he writes an "inspirational sermon." Then a curious thing happens. He has received hope from Hester. He transfers this hope for the future into religious terms. On the way to deliver the Election Sermon he is so spiritually exalted that he does not even notice Hester as he passes her. Hester knows that she has helped place him in this inspirational mood. She somewhat resents his inability to acknowledge her. On the day before his departure for the Old World and a new life, Dimmesdale arrives at the high point of his religious career—the delivery of the Election Sermon. His pride causes him to want this highest of honors accorded to Puritan ministers. Very likely, his preparation for the sermon has so inspired him that he then finds the courage to confess his share of Hester Prynne's sin.

After his confession he dies a happy man, in that he feels he is now acceptable in God's eyes. His hypocrisy should be forgiven (according to Puritan doctrines) because he has humbled himself and revealed his sin. Hester Prynne has won her peace of mind by being forced to submit publicly to people's harsh criticism. Dimmesdale wins his peace finally by a comparable revelation of his part in the sin.

ROGER CHILLINGWORTH

The villain of the story, Roger Chillingworth, makes his first appearance in Chapter III. He is seen by Hester Prynne when she is on the scaffold fulfilling her penance. He is described as if she were talking to herself in a hurried manner. First, she notes a "white man, clad in a strange disarray of civilized and savage costume," standing on the edge of the crowd. He is short and has a wrinkled brow. There is a "remarkable intelligence in his features." One of his shoulders rises higher than the other. He is not yet old enough to be termed "aged." For some time in the story, he is called the "stranger." Later, he takes the name "Roger Chillingworth," though he actually is Dr. Prynne, Hester's husband. In Europe he studied alchemy; in the American wilderness he has experimented with herbs used by the Indians. Thus, he is able to fit nicely into the Puritan community as a doctor (he is sometimes referred to as the "leech"). In the prison, he tries to force Hester to tell him the name of her lover. This she will not do. He then promises vengeance on the soul of the unknown man, the father of Pearl. He says he will not prosecute Hester; he will let the scarlet letter on her bosom do that for him. As time passes, Roger Chillingworth's physical appearance changes for the worse. Hester sees him at Governor Bellingham's mansion. His features have become "uglier"; his dark complexion has become "duskier"; and his figure has become even more "misshapen." After Dimmesdale offers his series of logical reasons why Pearl should not be removed from Hester's care, Chillingworth throws out his first remark to the minister, which suggests that the physician begins to suspect that the minister is the guilty man he is searching for. He says that Dimmesdale speaks "with a strange earnestness." Chapter IX, "The Leech," explains much about Chillingworth. He becomes the minister's physician. The two men spend much time together walking and talking. Chillingworth moves into the same house with Dimmesdale and sets up a laboratory.

In Chapter X, "The Leech and His Patient," the two men are in conversation about sin and the value of confession. Subtly, the physician points out to Dimmesdale that a "false show" (hiding sin) must not be preferred to "God's own truth" (confession). At this time, little Pearl sees Chillingworth and calls him the "old Black Man." (This expression is often used for Chillingworth when Pearl speaks of him later in the tale.) When the "leech" sees Dimmesdale's breast, with the red, unhealed wound in the flesh, he resembles Satan in great joy looking at a lost soul entering his kingdom of hell. This same look of the "arch-fiend" is repeated when Chillingworth stands in the marketplace in the middle of the night, observing Pearl with her mother and father. The light of the meteor reveals Chillingworth's expression—first a smile, then a scowl. The physician guesses at the state of mind that sends Dimmesdale out into the night. Hypocritically, he cautions Dimmesdale about studying too many books that trouble his brain, causing him to wander about in the night.

When Hester Prynne decides that she must talk with Chillingworth about Dimmesdale, she goes to meet him by the seashore. She notes that in seven years he has lost his "studious" appearance and has taken on an "eager, searching, almost fierce, yet carefully guarded look." He covers this expression "with a smile." Sometimes a "glare of red light" gleams out of his eyes. He has changed himself "into a devil" by "devoting himself to the constant analysis of a heart full of torture." He has enjoyed this analysis, gloating all the while. Telling Hester how he feels about Dimmesdale, he describes himself as a "fiend." He feels it is his "fate" to torment the minister. After he leaves Hester, she looks after him and declares aloud how she hates him, for he has done her "worse wrong" than she had done him. She believes that he, an older man, should never have married her, a young woman.

Hester reveals to Arthur the identity of his false friend. Then Dimmesdale makes a dramatic statement about the fiendish Chillingworth: "That old man's revenge has been blacker than my sin. He has violated, in cold blood, the sanctity of a human heart." (Most readers agree with the minister that the sin of revenge, an act of intellectual pride, is worse than the sin of hypocrisy.)

Chillingworth is last seen when, at the edge of the scaffold, he tries to prevent Dimmesdale from making a public confession. Dimmesdale calls him "tempter," declaring that he will "escape" him. When the determined minister mounts the steps of the scaffold, he is followed by Chillingworth who has been so closely "connected with the drama of guilt and sorrow" that he seems "entitled . . . to be present at its closing scene." After Dimmesdale confesses and dies, Roger Chillingworth loses his purpose in life. Within the year, Chillingworth—the avenger, the "fiend"—dies, leaving considerable property in Europe and America to Pearl. Dimmesdale, dying on the scaffold, cries out that God has shown mercy toward him, by sending Chillingworth, that "dark and terrible old man, to keep the torture always at red-heat!"

PEARL

Descriptions of little Pearl, Hester Prynne's child of sin, form a rich part of the story. With rare exception, wherever the mother is found, the child is also there. (The very first picture one has of Hester is in Chapter II, when the town official escorts her from the prison so that the townspeople might see her. Pearl is there also—"a baby of some three months old," winking and turning her little face from the bright sun.) As Pearl grows older, her mother dresses her in "fanciful" clothing of bright colors, adding to the strange charm the child already possesses. In Chapter VI, "Pearl," there is a full-length picture of young Pearl. She is described as a "lovely . . . flower," having sprung from a "guilty passion." Little Pearl has beauty; she has intelligence; she has physical gracefulness. Her mother has named her Pearl, "as being of great price . . . her mother's only treasure!" If she is crossed in any way, the child flies into a passion. She obeys no rules unless she wishes to do so. Her moods change quickly. At one moment, she is wild, desperate, defiant, and filled with bad temper and gloom; then, suddenly, she can change into the sunny, happy child who wants to assure her mother of her love by kissing and caressing her. Pearl seems to have no set standard to govern her own behavior—she reacts according to her particular feeling of the moment. She has a "certain peculiar look" on her face that sometimes causes Hester to question whether Pearl is a "human child" or a being from another world (like a "little elf"). Her eyes are "wild, bright, deeply-black." She is described as an "imp of evil, emblem and product of sin." The Puritan children flee in fear when resentful Pearl chases after them, flinging stones and shrill words at them. She is in as much social isolation as that in which her mother finds herself.

Once, Hester is frightened when she looks into the "mirror of Pearl's eyes." She sees a "freakish, elfish" look there; then, she believes she sees a "face, fiend-like, full of smiling malice" peeping out at her. In the headpiece of the armor in Governor Bellingham's hall, Hester is disturbed to see Pearl's expression, as it is reflected in the metal mirror. The child has an "elfish" look of "naughty merriment," as if an "imp" were "seeking to mould itself into Pearl's shape." Attracted by the brightness of her mother's scarlet letter, the three-year-old Pearl plays games, flinging wildflowers at her mother's symbol of sin. When Pearl playfully declares that she has "no Heavenly Father," Hester remembers that some of the townspeople regard Pearl as an offspring of the devil.

When Pearl is seven years old, she joins hands with her mother and father on the scaffold in the middle of the night. At this time, she asks the minister if he will join hands with her mother and her in the daylight of the next day. It is Pearl who points her finger toward Roger Chillingworth, making him a part of the dramatic scene, when the meteor reveals his presence nearby. (She often acts as a linking character, connecting different combinations of people through her childlike, penetrating comments, such as her comment that her mother wears the scarlet letter for the same reason that the "minister keeps his hand over his heart.") Consider Pearl as an influence on her mother's conduct; for example, Hester without a helpless child to protect and guide might not accept her punishment quite so passively as she seems to.

Sometimes Pearl is fanciful to the point that she is almost amusing. For instance, while her mother talks with Roger Chillingworth near the seashore, the imaginative child makes herself a mermaid's costume out of seaweed. Then, as a crowning touch, she gathers some eel grass and makes for herself a green letter *A*, imitating as closely as possible her mother's scarlet letter. Pearl often plays in the sunshine; in contrast, the sunshine will not shine directly on Hester. The child is so close to nature that the little animals in the forest scene, such as partridges, pigeons, and squirrels, almost completely ignore her when she is passing by them. They recognize a "wildness in the human child" comparable to their own. During the interview in the forest between Hester and Arthur, the mother calls Pearl to her side. The child refuses to come near her mother, because she misses the sight of the scarlet letter that Hester has cast off. Hester replaces the letter and the child joins her. How interesting this scene is, for the child and the letter parallel each other; both represent the mother's sin—the child being a physical representation and the scarlet letter being a symbol.

During the festivities of the New England Holiday, it is Pearl who describes Dimmesdale. She remarks that in the dark nighttime and in the forest he is one type of person (friendly and loving); in the "sunny day," he is a different sort of man, for he does not know them. She remarks, "A strange, sad man is he, with his hand always over his heart!" (Pearl is a very sympathetic person in that she does sense unusual aspects of situations, such as Dimmesdale's different behavior in different places.) As the story nears its conclusion, there is little dialogue from Pearl, who senses situations through intuition (that is, knowledge without reasoning). At the end of the tale, most of the threads of the plot are unraveled: Dimmesdale learns Chillingworth's identity; Hester plans to escape with her lover and her child; Dimmesdale confesses his sin. Pearl, by instinct, has supposed some things to be true that are true. At the end of the story, the duties of Pearl, Hester's "messenger of anguish," seem to be at an end. Chillingworth has left Pearl a considerable amount of property in England and in America. She is wealthy. The close of the tale finds Pearl far from Boston, no longer with her mother, very likely happily married with a child of her own.

MINOR CHARACTERS

All of Hawthorne's works of long fiction feature four main characters—two men and two women. Although the reader often has the feeling that the story involves many people, when a list of characters is made there are found to be very few characters except the main four. (Hawthorne gives the impression of large numbers by including people in crowd scenes, such as in processions and groups of townspeople.)

Mistress Hibbins is perhaps one of the most interesting of the minor characters in *The Scarlet Letter*. She is Governor Bellingham's "bitter-tempered sister," who a few years after the main action of the story is "executed as a witch." The "witch-lady," Mistress Hibbins, often talks of a "merry company in the forest" that meets at night with the "Black Man." Mistress Hibbins is a very specialized type of character, for she is a caricature type. (A caricature is a picture or description in which physical features, personality, or dress are so exaggerated that an absurd effect is produced.) In the matter of physical appearance, Governor Bellingham's sister looks like many other people. It is in the matter of her dress and personality (revealed through her actions) that she differs. Whenever she meets Hester Prynne, she feels called upon to invite Hester to join the Black Man and his company in the forest. Her repeated invitation forms a tag line; that is, a speech that the reader begins to associate with her. (Compare this with tag lines used by theater and television actors, who identify themselves for an audience by having their own special catchwords or phrases.) Each character in the story views what he or she sees or hears in the light of his own experience. In Chapter XII, when Mistress Hibbins hears Dimmesdale's cry in the night (from the scaffold), she thinks she is hearing the cries of "fiends and night-hags" with whom she is said to associate during her midnight excursions into the forest. One of the most dramatic scenes, in which the "sour and discontented" Mistress Hibbins takes part, occurs at the time when Dimmesdale returns from his forest interview with Hester (in Chapter XX). She accuses the minister of returning from a meeting with the Black Man of the forest. He explains that he has been visiting his pious friend, John Eliot (which is, to some extent, true). She answers to the effect that he lies very well. Mistress Hibbins sees Dimmesdale in the procession and confides to Hester that the pious minister in the procession is very much of a contrast with the Arthur Dimmesdale she knows who dances during the forest festivities of the Black Man. The governor's sister points out to Hester that she wears her scarlet letter "openly," but that Dimmesdale "seeks to hide" something "with his hand over his heart." Another aspect of Mistress Hibbins as a caricature character is the matter of her choice of clothing. She lives among Puritan folk who by law are required to wear somber clothing. (Even the magistrates wear their rich garments only at important ceremonial occasions.) At least twice, Mistress Hibbins is seen gorgeously dressed. First, she is seen by Dimmesdale on his return from the forest. She makes a "very grand appearance; having on a high head-dress, a rich gown of velvet, and a ruff done up with . . . yellow starch." During the New England Holiday festivities, she is seen "arrayed in great magnificence, with a triple ruff, a broidered stomacher, a gown of rich velvet, and a gold-headed cane." (A "ruff" is a wheel-shaped stiff collar, worn by men and women in Puritan times; a "stomacher" is the heavily embroidered or jeweled front part of a garment worn by elaborately dressed women of Mistress Hibbins's day.) Both through her actions and her speech, Governor Bellingham's sister, Mistress Hibbins, is a caricature. She adds variety and color to the story; because her comments do not necessarily need to be logical in their content, she is allowed to react instinctively (and sometimes correctly) to the other characters.

Governor Bellingham represents the law. A chief magistrate, he is seen first when Hester is brought to the scaffold for her penance. He is on the balcony, surrounded by representatives of the state and church. He wears a "dark feather in his hat, a border of embroidery on his cloak, and a black velvet tunic beneath." He is a man "advanced in years, with . . . hard experience written in his wrinkles"—a man well suited to be the "head and representative" of the Boston community. (Because he is the governor, and because he represents the authority of the community on special occasions, he is particularly elaborately dressed.) The governor's mansion, which Hester and Pearl visit, is a spacious, stucco-covered building. The furnishings in the main hall resemble those found in houses of wealthy gentlemen in England. The suit of armor on the wall was made for Governor Bellingham the same year that he left London to come to New England. He is proud of his garden and takes pleasure in showing it off to visitors, as he does when the Reverends John Wilson and Arthur Dimmesdale, and Roger Chillingworth visit him. The governor is very interested in religious matters and feels it his duty to instruct Reverend Wilson to question Pearl closely regarding her home training in religion. When Pearl refuses to answer his questions, the governor is greatly disturbed; he is finally satisfied when Reverend Dimmesdale explains to him that the child will be a great help in saving Hester from more sin. At the end of the story, Governor Bellingham is seen in the procession with the other magistrates. He and his fellow magistrates are described as being men of good size, physically, as well as men of "self-reliance." Governor Bellingham is a relatively kindly man of authority who represents the authority of the state, as compared with Reverends Dimmesdale and Wilson, who represent the authority of the church.

The Reverend John Wilson is the oldest of the group of ministers in Boston. He is a "great scholar" and a "man of kind and genial spirit." Beneath the edge of his skull cap peeps out a "border of grizzled locks." An intelligent man, he is more used to the "shaded light of his study" than the bright sunshine of the day. His fame as a scholar has not prepared him for the problems connected with "human guilt, passion, and anguish." Reverend Wilson persuades Dimmesdale to speak to Hester on the scaffold, to see if she will reveal the name of her lover. The next time Reverend Wilson is seen is when Hester goes to Governor Bellingham's mansion to protest the possibility of Pearl being taken from her. Mr. Wilson is being shown the governor's garden along with Dimmesdale and Chillingworth. When Pearl resists the governor's attempts to question her, Wilson tries. He is a "grandfatherly" sort of person, being "usually a vast favorite with children." But Pearl does not respond to him. Dimmesdale saves the day (at Hester's urgent request) when he explains the role that Pearl might play in helping Hester keep free from more sin. In Chapter XII, there is a brief picture of Wilson as he walks alone in the middle of the night, lighting himself home by the rays from a "glimmering lantern." He is returning from Governor Winthrop's death bed. The last view of John Wilson is after the Election Sermon, when he offers his arm to Dimmesdale as the procession is on its way from the meeting house to the town hall. Dimmesdale repels the "old man's arm" and totters on alone. This last action of the "venerable" pastor is typical of him. He has always been essentially kindly and often has put out his hand to help people. In contrast to the meanness, severity, and hypocrisy of many of the Puritans, the Reverend John Wilson is a man of great mercy and kindness.

CRITICAL COMMENTARY

Literary critics agree that *The Scarlet Letter* is Hawthorne's finest and most important work. Any major criticism of Hawthorne necessarily must have reference to his famous tale of Hester Prynne and her scarlet *A*. The first part of this summary of criticism deals with important references to Hawthorne and his entire work, which should enrich one's understanding of *The Scarlet Letter*. The second part is concerned especially with detailed studies of this particular novel.

IMPORTANT GENERAL CRITICISM

Nathaniel Hawthorne's son, Julian, wrote two helpful biographical works: *Nathaniel Hawthorne and His Wife: A Biography* and *Hawthorne and His Circle*. An important early work, which discusses Hawthorne as an unworldly writer, constantly using his own New England Puritan background, is Henry James's *Hawthorne*. A very fine study of Hawthorne is G. E. Woodberry's *Nathaniel Hawthorne*. Scarlet Letter themes are emphasized, such as the "recurring idea of isolation, the sense of secrecy in men's bosoms." Hawthorne's "inheritance from Puritanism" includes his "absorption in the moral sphere." Newton Arvin's *Hawthorne* discusses the novelist's great concern with guilt from the point of view of modern psychology. Arvin suggests that this idea comes from Hawthorne's own struggles during his lifetime, rather than from the Puritans. Randall Stewart's important *Nathaniel Hawthorne: A Biography* offers a picture of a more well-rounded person than had been seen in the older biographies. Two books that are quite light reading—and that offer much food for thought about Hawthorne's family background, including Puritanism—are Louise H. Tharp, *The Peabody Sisters of Salem,* and Vernon Loggins, *The Hawthornes: The Story of Seven Generations of an American Family*.

Concerning Hawthorne's ideas, especially Puritanism and literary form, the following three works are helpful. Austin

Warren's "Introduction" to his *Nathaniel Hawthorne: Representative Selections* discusses such aspects as "Theology," "The Problem of Sin," and "Hawthorne as Artist." There are illuminating, analytical comments on *The Scarlet Letter* (concerning literary form) in F. O. Matthiessen's *American Renaissance: Art and Expression in the Age of Emerson and Whitman.* Randall Stewart has a fascinating introduction to his edition of *The American Notebooks of Nathaniel Hawthorne;* one thoughtful section is "The Development of Character Types in Hawthorne's Fiction."

Some discussions about Hawthorne's religious beliefs have emphasized his point of view toward Puritanism. W. C. Brownell, in "Hawthorne," in *American Prose Masters,* believes Hawthorne succeeds only when he is concerned with Puritan themes. He calls *The Scarlet Letter* "the Puritan *Faust."* G. E. Woodberry's article "The Literary Age of Boston" analyzes Hawthorne not as someone who believes in the doctrines of Puritanism but as someone who has inherited the moral atmosphere of this faith. This helps explain Hawthorne's repeated emphasis on the pessimistic aspects of life. H. W. Schneider, in *The Puritan Mind,* sees Hawthorne as someone who "understood" Puritanism. F. I. Carpenter, in "The Puritans Preferred Blondes: The Heroines of Melville and Hawthorne," discusses Hawthorne's attitude toward several Puritan points of view on freedom and sin. Barriss Mills, in "Hawthorne and Puritanism," discusses some aspects of Puritanism that Hawthorne approved of, such as justice, courage, and seriousness.

Considering Hawthorne's social and political ideas, much has been written. N. F. Doubleday, in "Hawthorne's Hester and Feminism," reviews *The Scarlet Letter* and decides that Hawthorne is not in accord with the midnineteenth-century point of view toward women's rights. It is suggested that Hawthorne saw the feminist movement as not being truly aware of the actual nature of woman and her role in the world.

In regard to Hawthorne's literary theory, as it applies to *The Scarlet Letter,* examine Charles Foster, "Hawthorne's Literary Theory," especially with reference to symbolism. Hawthorne's own theory of romance is somewhat explored in "The Custom House," the introductory sketch for his 1850 romance. The "Preface" to *The House of the Seven Gables* includes the famous passage concerning the management of the "atmospherical medium." The "Preface" to Hawthorne's *Blithedale Romance* mentions the romancer's choice of a suitable setting as being one somewhat separated from the ordinary pathway. Hawthorne's "Preface" to *The Marble Faun* analyzes the necessary requirements for the proper setting of one of his romances.

The sources of Hawthorne's works have stimulated much critical inquiry. Randall Stewart's introduction to *The American Notebooks* states that Hawthorne used three sources for his writings: his own journals, his varied reading, and his own fiction. Arlin Turner, in "Hawthorne's Methods of Using His Source Materials," presents an examination of Hawthorne's journals and some of the completed works based on the journal entries. Turner states that Hawthorne began with a "central theme or basic idea" and then backed up this idea with numerous examples as dramatized illustrations, sometimes in the form of "catalogues" (listings of items) or "processions" (the bringing together of numerous important key people, such as the procession during the New England holiday in *The Scarlet Letter*). J. E. Hart's "*The Scarlet Letter:* One Hundred Years After" suggests that Hawthorne's characters represent varied facets of his own character. A study of the Gothic influence is N. F. Doubleday's "Hawthorne's Use of Three Gothic Patterns," which investigates mysterious portraits, witchcraft, and the elixir of life (the fountain of youth liquid). W. B. Stein's *Hawthorne's Faust: A Study of the Devil Archetype* emphasizes the role of evil in the works (check this for references to the "fiend" Chillingworth).

CRITICISM WITH SPECIAL REFERENCE TO THE SCARLET LETTER

There has been much criticism of *The Scarlet Letter.* One prominent reviewer of Hawthorne's own day, E. P. Whipple, reviewed it in *Graham's Magazine.* Whipple admired Hawthorne's keenness of vision, his originality, his powers of observation, and his character portrayals. G. P. Lathrop's *A Study of Hawthorne* is sensitively alert to the relationships of characters to theme. Anthony Trollope, in "The Genius of Nathaniel Hawthorne," refers to Hawthorne's "weird, mysterious, thrilling charm." Henry James's *Hawthorne* contains a fine commentary on *The Scarlet Letter.* James criticizes Hawthorne for what he calls the use of too many symbols. W. C. Brownell's "Hawthorne" in his *American Prose Masters* is highly complimentary about *The Scarlet Letter* (although he criticizes Hawthorne's other works for what he called the poor use of allegory). Yvor Winters in *In Defense of Reason* refers to *The Scarlet Letter* as a marvelous work due to its use of allegory concerning colonial New England. He feels, however, that Hawthorne's themes and characters are not truly significant. F. O. Matthiessen's *American Renaissance* is very fine for its perceptive interpretations of *The Scarlet Letter.* An unusual work of criticism is Leland Schubert's *Hawthorne, the Artist: Fine-Art Devices in Fiction,* which deals with the form of the works, not their contents. He selects artistic devices used by painters and composers (such as color, sound, and rhythmic motifs) and locates devices parallel to these in Hawthorne's fiction. He looks at *The Scarlet Letter* as a three-part work, based on the three scaffold scenes. Another approach is the seven-part division, determined by the characters and their activities in certain chapters. The "recurring use of melodies and chords" of music is compared to "repeated . . . words and phrases, or colors" in a novel. Mark Van Doren's *Hawthorne* emphasizes the place of allegory in Hawthorne. R. H. Fogel's *Hawthorne's Fiction: The Light and the Dark* points out the strong element of contrast of light (or color) in *The Scarlet Letter.* John C. Gerber's "Form and

Content in *The Scarlet Letter*" suggests that the novel is divided into four parts, with each part being individualized by a character who is either involved with or responsible for the action of that part. The divisions are as follows: the community (and the four major characters) in Chapters I–VIII; Chillingworth in Chapters IX–XII; Hester Chapters XIII–XX; and Dimmesdale in Chapters XXI–XXIV. A very worthy work of criticism is C. C. Walcutt's "*The Scarlet Letter* and Its Modern Critics." Walcutt surveys the varied interpretations of the book under the headings of orthodox Puritan, romantic, transcendental, and relativist. He discusses why there is such variance as he analyzes the symbolism, the way Hawthorne views his sinful characters, the frequent identification of readers with various characters, and Hawthorne's basic contradiction of attitude concerning sin and Providence.

ESSAY QUESTIONS AND ANSWERS

QUESTION

Name a few of the themes or basic ideas Hawthorne introduces in *The Scarlet Letter* and show how he develops them.

ANSWER

Basic to an understanding of this work is the knowledge that Hawthorne is not exalting and praising Puritanism and that his romance is a detailed criticism of the Puritan way of life. He is building up an elaborate picture to show his contempt for a society that could be so intensely intolerant of individuals and their slips from the path of virtue. The women in Chapter II (to the best of our knowledge, representative of Boston womanhood) are vicious in their criticism of Hester. They regret she is not to die or, at least, to be branded on the forehead with a hot iron. (These women match the three witches in Shakespeare's *Macbeth* in unattractiveness of personality.) Consider Hester's good deeds to the poor (nursing and sewing); the very ones she helps generally throw bitter words in her face. Later in her life, Hester is a respected member of the community, for the passage of time and her continued good deeds help many people to forget her sin of adultery.

To an extent, Chillingworth represents pride of intellect. He is a scientist-physician, proud of his achievements. When he finds Hester in her distressed condition on the scaffold, he rejects her. His pride is hurt. Here is a struggle between the head (study, reflection, and speculation) and the heart (his former affection for Hester). If he were to allow his heart to win the struggle, he might still be capable of future happiness. But, as is often the case with the scientist, says Hawthorne, he brings suffering on himself because of his disregard of the basic laws of human affection and brotherhood.

A major theme in Hawthorne's works is the evil of isolation;

that is, being separated from others physically, socially, mentally, or morally. Because of her sin of adultery, Hester Prynne is isolated from Boston society. She lives in a cottage separated from others in the community. She is not allowed to sew certain objects (such as new bride's veils), for her tainted hands would soil them. She has no idle chatter with others. She is either ignored or taunted by parents and children alike. But through her admission of her sin, and by her good works, she is partially redeemed and is readmitted into society. Many examples could be cited to point out the isolation of Dimmesdale (secretly suffering from remorse and a bad conscience) and Chillingworth (eagerly pursuing the victim of his revenge). Even Pearl, the product of the sin that has caused the various types of isolation, is isolated, not only from other children, but also from her mother (to a great extent) and from her father (until near the end of the story).

Guilt that is admitted openly, such as Hester's daily wearing of her scarlet symbol, eventually is cleansed out of the system. Guilt that is hidden, such as Dimmesdale's, succeeds only in exciting remorse, a bad conscience, and eventual hypocrisy. The Puritan belief in confession as a means of purifying the soul applies here. Hester's wearing of the letter is a daily confession. She suffers less and less as time goes on. People begin to forget her past difficulties. In contrast to this, Dimmesdale has not confessed, and his troubled conscience bothers him almost as much as the "red stigma" (unhealed wound on his breast) over which he often places his hand. Actually, Hester's wearing the scarlet letter does not make her truly regretful of her sin as it is supposed to do. It only makes her submissive, and the Puritan community is happy and contented that it has the upper hand over her. In like fashion, Dimmesdale's "red stigma" represents his deep regret for the sin, but it is not a proper substitute for public confession.

QUESTION

Show how Hawthorne in *The Scarlet Letter* uses names of people who actually lived to give added meaning to his story.

ANSWER

Two of the characters who appear in the story did live in Boston in the 1640s and 1650s. They are the Reverend John Wilson and Governor Bellingham. Hawthorne identifies John Wilson as "the eldest clergyman of Boston, a great scholar . . . and withal a man of kind and genial spirit." Colonial histories help support this complimentary picture of the famous clergyman. He and Arthur Dimmesdale are fellow workers in the area of religion. Hawthorne's romance, half-way between the worlds of reality and imagination, thus has one fine example of reality (Wilson) placed beside an unusual creation of the imagination (Dimmesdale). The other character who actually lived in Boston is Governor Bellingham. The Boston community is ruled by a combination of the church (Wilson, Dimmesdale, and the other ministers) and the state (the magistrates, especially Governors Bellingham and Winthrop). This is called a theocratic state.

Five individuals are merely mentioned in the story, but each adds a special flavor of his or her own to the tale. They are Ann Hutchinson, Governor Winthrop, John Eliot, Sir Thomas Overbury, and Ann Turner. The use of Ann Hutchinson's name at the end of the first chapter foreshadows (looks forward to) certain aspects of Hester Prynne later in the novel. Ann Hutchinson, who disturbed the Puritan authorities a few years before Hester Prynne's time, was an early feminist, a fighter for women's rights. Hester, occupying the same prison that had once confined Ann Hutchinson, throughout the story— and especially in the next-to-last paragraph of the work—is concerned with a "new truth" about the "relation between man and woman." The early mention of Ann Hutchinson pre-pares our minds for the kind of woman Hester might have developed into if she had not been forced to wear the scarlet letter. Governor Winthrop is not seen in the story, but the fact that the seven-year-old Pearl has been with her mother at his deathbed helps us decide the definite date of the beginning of the novel. He died in 1649. Hester first stands on the scaffold in 1642. Hester came to America in 1640, two years before this time.

The Apostle Eliot also lived at this time. Dimmesdale told Mistress Hibbins he had been to see him in the forest. Ann Turner, the "especial friend" of Mistress Hibbins (mentioned in Chapter XX), had taught the witch lady the secret of doing up the ruff around her neck with yellow starch. Ann was hanged "for Sir Thomas Overbury's murder." (There was a famous trial in England over the death of Overbury in 1613.) Following the old maxim that "birds of a feather flock together," one sees another aspect of Mistress Hibbins's already darkened personality—she is the "especial friend" of a murderess.

QUESTION

Hawthorne probably used more mirrors for literary purposes than anyone else in American literature. Point out the mirrors in *The Scarlet Letter* and suggest briefly how several of them are used.

ANSWER

Chapter II: Hester, on the scaffold, remembers "her own face . . . illuminating all the interior of the dusky mirror in which she had been wont to gaze at it." Chapter VI: Hester sees in little Pearl a "shadowy reflection of the evil . . . in herself." Hester looks at "her own image" in the eyes of Pearl; then she sees "another face, in the small black mirror of Pearl's eye." Chapter VII: Pearl looks into the "polished mirror of the breastplate" of the suit of armor in Governor Bellingham's hall. Hester looks, and she sees that "owing to the peculiar effect of this convex mirror, the scarlet letter" is "represented in exaggerated and gigantic proportions." (The rounded-out mirrored surface creates a strange, exaggerated effect.) Pearl's "look of naughty merriment" is "likewise in the mirror" of the headpiece of the suit of armor. Chapter XI: Often at night, Dimmesdale views "his own face in a looking-glass," by the "most powerful light" that he can throw upon it. (This is suggestive of his constant searching within himself, examining his bad conscience.) Sometimes "visions" would "flit before him . . . within the looking-glass." Chapter XIV: Pearl peeps "curiously into a pool, left by the retiring tide as a mirror . . . to see her face in." There peeps at her "out of the pool . . . the image of a little maid," whom Pearl invites "to take her hand, and run a race with her." This scene helps further accent Pearl's "selfish" personality. Beside the seashore, Chillingworth describes to Hester how he has tortured Dimmesdale. "The unfortunate physician, while uttering these words," lifts "his hands with a look of horror," as if he is viewing "some frightful shape" that he cannot recognize, "usurping the place of his own image in a glass." (This is an instance of self-revelation through the mirror image.) Chapter XV: At the edge of the seashore, Pearl flirts "fancifully with her own image in a pool of water, beckoning the phantom forth." Finding that "either she or the image" is "unreal," she turns to other activities. Chapter XVI: In the forest, Hester and Pearl watch the "reflected light" on the surface of the water. They wonder if the "old forest" might "mirror" its strange tales "on the smooth surface of a pool." Chapter XIX: While Pearl waits for her mother and Dimmesdale to finish talking in the forest, she stands by the brook, which chances "to form a pool, so smooth and quiet" that "reflected" in the still water is a "perfect image of her figure . . . but more refined and spiritualized than the reality." The "image" seems "to communicate somewhat of its own shadowy and intangible quality to the child itself." When Pearl points her finger toward Hester's breast, where the scarlet letter has been, there, "beneath, in the mirror of the brook," is the "image of little Pearl, pointing her small forefinger too." Pearl becomes angry. "In the brook . . . is the fantastic beauty of the image, with its reflected frown, its pointed finger, and

imperious gesture, giving emphasis to the aspect of little Pearl."
Then Pearl bursts into a "fit of passion," and "in the brook,
once more," is the "shadowy wraith of Pearl's image." (Hester,
disturbed at Pearl's behavior, is upset at seeing both the child
and her fantastic reflection.) Chapter XXI: The festivities of
the "New England Holiday" are a "dim reflection of a remem-
bered splendor." The activities centering around "the annual
installation of magistrates" do not really compare with the
magnificent displays in London at a "Lord Mayor's show."

QUESTION

Describe various aspects of Puritanism pictured in *The Scarlet
Letter*.

ANSWER

Hawthorne is very concerned with the intolerance and
bigotry of his Puritan ancestors. In *The Scarlet Letter,* he
creates characters and situations to help project his complex
and ambiguous point of view about Puritan Boston. The story
is set in the 1640s and 1650s during the relatively early years
of the Boston colony. The early Puritans believe in a Trinity
with absolute power, controlling everything. People have no
real decisions to make concerning the world around them,
for God—at His whim—will decide. There is hope through
the sacrifice of the Christ. But not all people are to be saved.
The Doctrine of the Elect states that God chooses some for
heaven, and in the same manner allows others to go to hell.
One does not know if he or she is destined for heaven, but
generally—as in the case of Dimmesdale, the highly repu-
table Boston minister—there is a strong feeling that some
sainted individuals are certainly fated to go heavenward. In
The Scarlet Letter, part of Dimmesdale's torture is his knowledge of his own sin, which, unconfessed, will keep him from
heaven. Faithfulness between husband and wife is important.
Certainly a woman destined for heaven would never commit
adultery, as Hester Prynne does. She could not do so even if
she wished to, because her conduct is determined ahead of

time. Then too, Hester's and Arthur's actions are affected by predestination. Since Adam and Eve, we have lost the power to make decisions for ourselves, for, through "original sin" (disobedience to God's will in the Garden of Eden), man has lost the power of free will. God, the Absolute, makes all the decisions. Near the end of Chapter XIV, Chillingworth says to Hester that, since her "first step" in the wrong direction, "it has all been a dark necessity. . . . It has been our fate." He refers to the consequences of her action. Hester's disobedience to God's will is her act of adultery, a fearful word in Puritan days, for this act against fidelity in marriage endangers the very basis and strength of Puritan life. The Puritans are intolerant of anything they consider to be evil. Their community, Boston, is an experiment that the Christian world is watching with interest, so intolerance of evil must be their watchword. Hester is forced to openly accept her shame. Dimmesdale, her lover, is able to avoid public shame, but he cannot avoid great suffering, due to the awareness he has of his own hypocrisy, his own unworthiness.

Another aspect of Puritan thought is the source of God's will. It is in the Bible (the Scriptures). The Puritans distrust nature as a guide for behavior. (Hester and Dimmesdale feel free in the forest during their talk.) University-trained clergymen such as Dimmesdale, and Wilson from England, are highly respected, for they are able to interpret the meaning of the Bible. (Note the contrasting effect of the biblical scenes in the tapestry in Dimmesdale's apartment. David, Bathsheba, and Nathan the Prophet are not exactly representative of the Christian virtues of fidelity emphasized by the Puritans.) The Puritan belief that we are saved by faith, rather than by works, is seen in *The Scarlet Letter*. Over and over again, Hester aids those around her who need help. She especially makes great efforts to nurse and sew for the poor. Often this group repays her by taunting her with bitter words. In the official estimation of the Puritans, Hester has not advanced her standing by helping others. Actually, over a period of time, she has been able to reclaim much of her good name, for people finally begin to interpret her scarlet letter as meaning *A* for "Able" (or even "Angel").

The Puritans believe in the value of confession. The first members of the Boston Puritan church are required to make a public acknowledgment of their sins. (Later, the new members of the Puritan group are allowed to confess their sins in the privacy of the minister's study.) How Hester's scarlet symbol must delight her viewers, for she is constantly confessing to the world by displaying her letter of adultery! How unattractive to Dimmesdale must confession be! He can work himself into an emotional state in which he feels that at any moment he may confess (such as his humility in the pulpit, or his scream for attention on the scaffold in the middle of the night). But, having relieved his conscience to some extent by these long preparations, he then retreats from actually telling his sin. His hidden sin burns inside his breast. This remorse is intensified by the goading of Chillingworth, who has no real wish to reveal Dimmesdale as a sinner to his congregation. His wish is to torture him with thoughts of public shame if the sin is discovered.

Another angle of importance is the strong Puritan distrust of decisions reached only by the head; the Puritans feel the necessity of understanding being a result of spontaneous decision coming from the heart. Notice that Dimmesdale's great popularity as a speaker stems from his wonderful ability to excite the imagination, to fire the enthusiasm, of his hearers. Dimmesdale does not appeal solely to the mind—his greatest sermons speak to the heart. One sin strongly condemned by the Puritans is intellectual pride, the cause of Adam's fall and all our woe. How they admire the humility of Dimmesdale when from his pulpit he begins to paint a picture of himself as a miserable sinner! His unfinished confession causes them to exalt him and to examine over again their own many failings.

One very important aspect of Puritan society is its form of government—the theocratic state. In Boston, the church is so very important that it shares authority with the state in governing the colony. This procedure is based on the social order described in the Old Testament. Scholarly, university-trained ministers such as the Reverend John Wilson and the Reverend Arthur Dimmesdale interpret the Scriptures. The principle is the same as that established for the ancient biblical Covenant that assured obedience to properly elected leaders. These leaders could be displaced if they were unworthy. In the procession before the Election Sermon, Reverend Arthur Dimmesdale walks in the place of honor. His sermon is the high point of the entire "New England Holiday." Hawthorne chooses a wonderful method of showing his distrust of the Puritan way of life. He creates one of his major characters (Dimmesdale) as not only a highly respected member of the Puritan community but also as a weak and suffering hypocrite.

SUGGESTIONS FOR RESEARCH PAPER TOPICS

1. How has critical opinion changed over the last one hundred years concerning *The Scarlet Letter?* What are the main ideas explored in this romance? What aspects of Hawthorne's own personality are revealed in the book? How does this literary work differ from the works of others of the same period?

2. What was Hawthorne's point of view toward Puritanism? Did he approve or disapprove of it? Was he trying to prove something about Puritanism? How does Hawthorne use the elements of Puritanism to help make his story worthwhile and interesting?

3. What literary techniques did Hawthorne borrow from other writers? What ones did he discover for himself? How do his literary devices differ from those used by others who wrote at the same time?

4. How does Hawthorne adapt the European Gothic techniques to his fiction set in America? Do the techniques change? (For example, does a European castle become an old New England house?)

5. What does Hawthorne think of women's rights?

6. How does Hawthorne dramatize isolation and its effects in *The Scarlet Letter?*

7. How does Hawthorne weave witchcraft into his story? Does witchcraft add or detract from the general effectiveness of his fiction?

8. How does Hawthorne develop his characters? What are some of his techniques to make them seem like real-life characters? Are they walking symbols of various vices and virtues? Do their symbolic qualities detract from their reality?

9. What is the function of symbolism in *The Scarlet Letter?* Does Hawthorne's use of symbolism add or subtract from the story? How do the symbols help clarify the issues discussed about Puritanism? What are the various types of symbols used? What is the symbolism connected with "the light and the dark" scenes? How does Hawthorne use colors symbolically?

BIBLIOGRAPHY

Abel, Darrel. "Hawthorne's Hester." *College English*. 1952.

Arvin, Newton. *Hawthorne*. 1929.

Barnett, Louise K. "Speech and Society in *The Scarlet Letter*." *Emerson Society Quarterly*. 1983.

Bayer, John G. "Narrative Techniques and the Oral Tradition in *The Scarlet Letter*." *American Literature*. 1980.

Baym, Nina. The Scarlet Letter: *A Reading*. 1986.

————. *The Shape of Hawthorne's Career*. 1976.

Bell, Millicent. "The Obliquity of Signs: *The Scarlet Letter*." *Massachusetts Review*. 1982.

Bewley, Marius. "Hawthorne's Novels." *The Eccentric Design*. 1959.

Boewe, Charles, and Murray G. Murphy. "Hester Prynne in History." *American Literature*. 1960.

Broadhurst, Richard H. *Hawthorne, Melville and the Novel*. 1976.

Brooks, Van Wyck. *The Flowering of New England 1815–1865*. 1936.

Brownell, W. C. "Hawthorne." *American Prose Masters*. 1909.

Canaday, Nicholas. "Another Look at Arthur Dimmesdale." *CEA Critic*. 1979.

Cantwell, Robert. *Nathaniel Hawthorne: The American Years*. 1948.

Carpenter, F. I. "The Puritans Preferred Blondes: The Heroines of Melville and Hawthorne." *New England Quarterly*. 1936.

Colacurcio, Michael J., ed. *New Essays on The Scarlet Letter*. 1985.

Cowie, Alexander. "Nathaniel Hawthorne." *The Rise of the American Novel*. 1948.

Cowley, Malcom. "Five Acts of *The Scarlet Letter*." *College English*. 1957.

Cowley, Malcolm, ed. *The Portable Hawthorne*. 1948.

Cronin, Morton. "Hawthorne and Romantic Love and the Status of Women." Publications of the Modern Language Association. 1954.

Curtis, G. W. "The Works of Nathaniel Hawthorne." *North American Review*. 1864.

Dauber, Kenneth. *Rediscovering Hawthorne*. 1977.

Doubleday, N. F. "Hawthorne's Hester and Feminism." Publications of the Modern Language Association. 1939.

_____. "Hawthorne's Use of Three Gothic Patterns." *College English*. 1946.

Dryden, Edgar A. *Nathaniel Hawthorne: The Poetics of Enchantment*. 1977.

Eisinger, C. E. "Pearl and the Puritan Heritage." *College English*. 1951.

Feidelson, Charles Jr. "Hawthorne." *Symbolism in American Literature*. 1953.

Fleischmann, Fritz, ed. *American Novelists Revisited: Essays in Feminist Criticism.* 1982.

Fogle, R. H. *Hawthorne's Fiction: The Light and the Dark.* 1953.

Foster, Charles. "Hawthorne's Literary Theory." Publications of the Modern Language Association. 1942.

Fryer, Judith. *The Faces of Eve: Women in the Nineteenth-Century American Novel.* 1976.

Garlitz, Barbara. "Pearl: 1850–1955." Publications of the Modern Language Association. 1957.

Gerber, John C. "Form and Content in *The Scarlet Letter.*" *New England Quarterly.* 1944.

Golin, Rita K. *Nathaniel Hawthorne and the Truth of Dreams.* 1979.

Gorman, Herbert. *Hawthorne: A Study in Solitude.* 1927.

Hardwick, Elizabeth. *Seduction and Betrayal: Women in Literature.* 1974.

Hart, J. E. "*The Scarlet Letter:* One Hundred Years After." *New England Quarterly.* 1950.

Hawthorne, Julian. *Hawthorne and His Circle.* 1903.

_____. *Nathaniel Hawthorne and His Wife: A Biography.* 2 vols. 1884.

Hoeltje, Herbert H. "The Writing of *The Scarlet Letter.*" *New England Quarterly.* 1954.

Hoffman, Daniel G. *Fable and Form in American Fiction.* 1961.

James, Henry. *Hawthorne*. 1879.

Jehlen, Myra, ed. *American Incarnation: The Individual, the Nation and the Continent*. 1986.

Lathrop, G. P. *A Study of Hawthorne*. 1876.

Lawrence, D. H. "Hawthorne." *Studies in Classical American Literature*. 1923.

Lee, A. Robert, ed. *Nathaniel Hawthorne: New Critical Essays*. 1982.

Levin, Harry. "Hawthorne's Fiction." *The Power of Blackness: Hawthorne, Poe and Melville*. 1958.

Lewis, R. W. B. "The Return into Time: Hawthorne." *The American Adam: Innocence, Tragedy in the Nineteenth Century*. 1955.

Loggins, Vernon. *The Hawthornes: The Story of Seven Generations of an American Family*. 1951.

Male, Roy R. *Hawthorne's Tragic Vision*. 1957.

Matthiessen, F. O. *American Renaissance: Art and Expression in the Age of Emerson and Whitman*. 1941.

McNamara, Anne Marie. "The Character of Flame: The Function of Pearl in *The Scarlet Letter*." *American Literature*. 1956.

Mellow, James R. *Nathaniel Hawthorne in His Times*. 1980.

Miller, Edwin Haviland. *Salem Is My Dwelling Place: A Life of Nathaniel Hawthorne*. 1981.

Miller, Perry. *The New England Mind*. 1939.

Miller, Perry, and Thomas H. Johnson, eds. *The Puritans*. 1938.

Mills, Barriss. "Hawthorne and Puritanism." *New England Quarterly*. 1948.

Moers, Ellen. "*The Scarlet Letter:* A Political Reading." *Prospects*. 1985.

More, P. E. "The Solitude of Nathaniel Hawthorne." *Atlantic Monthly*. 1901.

Orians, G. H. "Hawthorne and Puritan Punishments." *College English*. 1952.

Quinn, Arthur Hobson, ed. *The Literature of the American People*. 1951.

Rahv, Phillip. "The Dark Lady of Salem." *Partisan Review*. 1941.

Ryskamp, Charles. "The New England Sources of *The Scarlet Letter*." *American Literature*. 1959.

Schneider, H. W. *The Puritan Mind*. 1930.

Schubert, Leland. *Hawthorne, the Artist: Fine-Art Devices in Fiction*. 1944.

Sherman, S. P. "Hawthorne: A Puritan Critic of Puritanism." *Americans*. 1922.

Snell, George. "Nathaniel Hawthorne, Bystander." *The Shapers of American Fiction, 1798–1947*. 1947.

Spiller, Robert E., et al., eds. *Literary History of the United States*. 1948.

Staal, Arie. *Hawthorne's Narrative Art.* 1976.

Stein, W. B. *Hawthorne's Faust: A Study of the Devil Archetype.* 1953.

Stewart, Randall. *Nathaniel Hawthorne: A Biography.* 1948.

Stewart, Randall, ed. *The American Notebooks of Nathaniel Hawthorne.* 1932.

Tharp, Louise H. *The Peabody Sisters of Salem.* 1950.

Turner, Arlin. "Hawthorne's Methods of Using His Source Materials." *Studies for W. A. Reed.* 1940.

Van Doren, Carl. "Flower of Puritanism: Hawthorne's *Scarlet Letter.*" *The Nation.* 1920.

_____. "Nathaniel Hawthorne." *The American Novel,* rev. ed. 1940.

Van Doren, Mark. *Hawthorne.* 1949.

Waggoner, Hyatt Howe. *Hawthorne: A Critical Study.* 1955.

_____. "Introduction." Nathaniel Hawthorne: *Selected Tales and Romances.* 1950.

_____. *The Presence of Hawthorne.* 1979.

Walcutt, C. C. "*The Scarlet Letter* and Its Modern Critics." *Nineteenth-Century Fiction.* 1953.

Warren, Austin. *Nathaniel Hawthorne: Representative Selections.* 1934.

_____. "Nathaniel Hawthorne." *Rage for Order.* 1948.

Whipple, E. P. "The Scarlet Letter" (review). *Graham's Magazine*. 1850.

Wilson, Edmund. *The Shock of Recognition*. 1943.

Winters, Yvor. *In Defense of Reason*. 1948.

Woodberry, G. E. "The Literary Age of Boston." *Harper's*. 1903.

_____. *Nathaniel Hawthorne*. 1902.